insight text guide

Sue Tweg

A Midsummer Night's Dream

William Shakespeare

First published in 2024.

Insight Publications Pty Ltd
3/350 Charman Road
Cheltenham VIC 3192
Australia
Tel: +61 3 8571 4950
Email: books@insightpublications.com.au

www.insightpublications.com.au

William Shakespeare's *A Midsummer Night's Dream* / Sue Tweg

Sue Tweg asserts the moral right to be identified as the author of this work.

ISBNs:
9781923016309 (print)
9781923016316 (digital)

Cover design by Hayley Sinnatt
Layout by Bec Yule @ Red Chilli Design
Edited by Robert Beardwood
Proofread by Kate McGregor

Printed by Markono Print Media Pte Ltd

Insight Publications acknowledges the Traditional Custodians of the Country on which we meet and work, the Boonwurrung People of the Kulin Nation. We pay our respects to their Elders past and present, and extend that respect to all Aboriginal and Torres Strait Islander peoples.

contents

Character map iv

Overview 1

About the author 1

Synopsis 2

Character summaries 5

Background & context 11

Genre, structure & language 14

Scene-by-scene analysis 17

Characters & relationships 33

Themes, ideas & values 43

Different interpretations 60

Questions & answers 64

Sample answer 72

References & reading 75

CHARACTER MAP

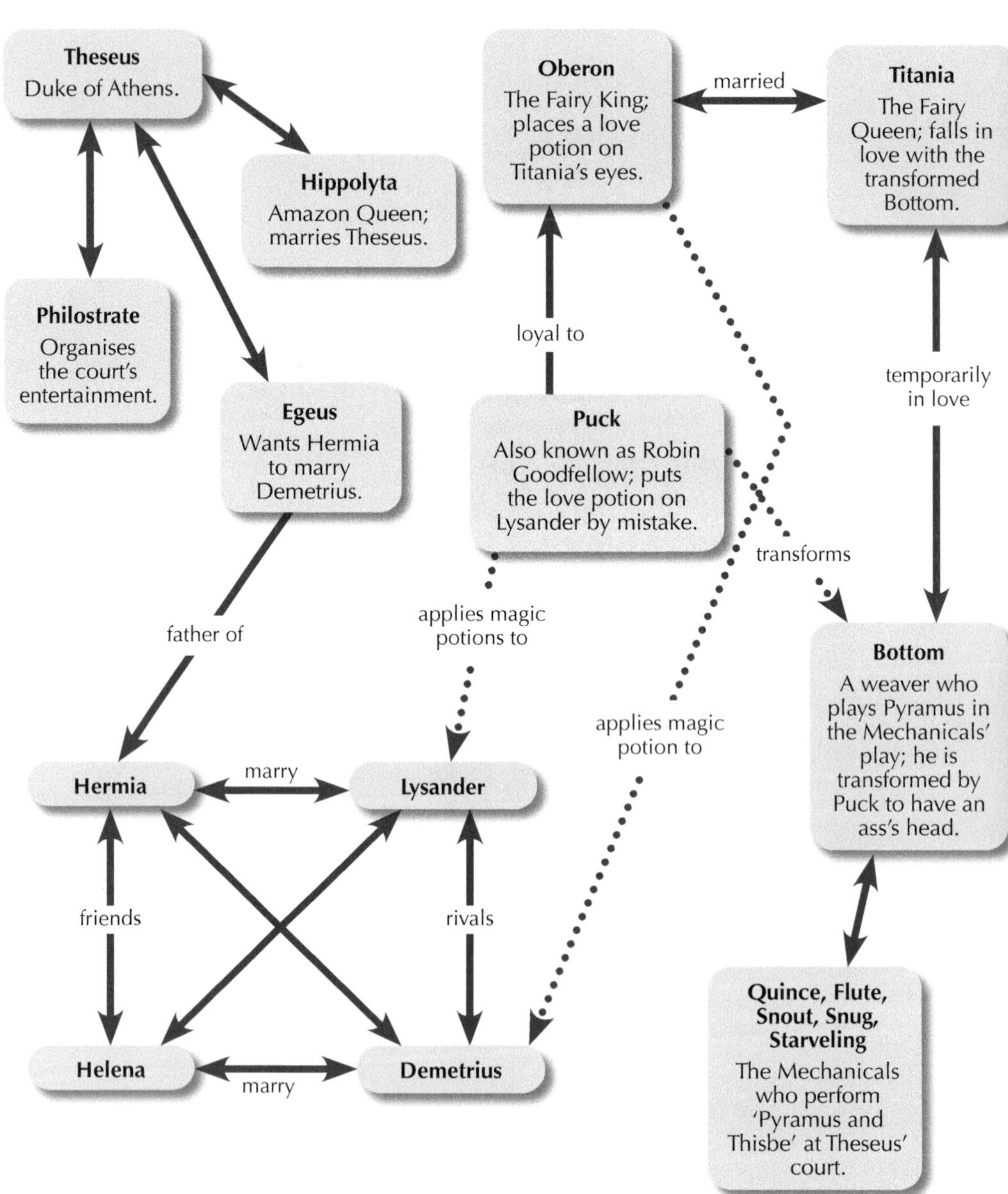

OVERVIEW

A book called *A mydsomer nights dreame* was entered into the London Stationers' Register (an early kind of copyright protection) in 1600. In the same year a printed Quarto (Q1) noted on its title page, 'As it hath been sundry times publickely acted, by the Right honourable, the Lord Chamberlaine his servants. Written by William Shakespeare'.

While we have no exact record of when *A Midsummer Night's Dream* was written, the statement that it was regularly acted before 1600 gives us a date around 1594–96, the same time as *Romeo and Juliet* was written. These are two of Shakespeare's best-known plays and they both take love as their motivating idea, one ending in tragedy, and the other a comedy ending in marriage for all the lovers.

A Midsummer Night's Dream is a clever and funny play, which works through mistaking and magic to explore the tangles anyone can get into when they fall in love. It always makes a theatre audience laugh and feel satisfied with the happy ending, but when we take time to look further into the play we see more complexity and encounter unsettling questions. Shakespeare never tells us what to think but explores the serious side of love and the often cruel or disappointing things that guarantee 'the path of true love never did run smooth'.

About the author

William Shakespeare was born in 1564 in Stratford-upon-Avon, a small country town in Warwickshire, England. At school he would have learned enough about Greek mythology and Roman history to imagine his own version of the classical hero Theseus. By the late 1580s he had moved to London, joined a company of actors and begun establishing himself as a playwright.

The range of Shakespeare's creative work shows that he was widely read in the classics, especially Ovid's *Metamorphoses* (written in Latin in 8 CE) and Plutarch's *Lives of the Noble Greeks and Romans* (written in Greek in the second century CE), both of which were translated into English as he was growing up. He also knew collections of European stories and was up to date with ideas, gossip and folklore in his own society. Shakespeare incorporated information from many sources into his plays and poems as well as inventing new plots out of well-known stories, combining and borrowing material as we see in *A Midsummer Night's Dream*.

Synopsis

Act 1

In Athens, Duke Theseus and Hippolyta, Queen of the Amazons, wait for their wedding at the new moon. They are interrupted by Egeus, Hermia's angry father, who demands that Theseus force his daughter to marry Demetrius, the young man of his choice, rather than her choice of Lysander, who loves her. Hermia and Lysander tell their friend Helena, who has been jilted by Demetrius, that they plan to escape the Athenian law by eloping at night through the wood outside the city. Helena decides to tell Demetrius, hoping she can win him back by following him when he goes in pursuit of Hermia.

Meanwhile, six local Athenian craftsmen, 'the Mechanicals', plan a dramatic entertainment for the royal wedding. They arrange to meet in the wood the following evening to rehearse their Interlude of 'Pyramus and Thisbe'.

Act 2

In the wood, a fairy and the trickster hobgoblin Puck describe the quarrel that has erupted between Oberon and Titania, king and queen of the fairies, for possession of a little Indian boy. Their discord has damaged the natural world but neither will give way. In revenge for Titania's disobedience, Oberon instructs Puck to find a magic herb that will enchant Titania's eyes when she is asleep, so that she will fall instantly in love with the first thing she sees when she wakes up. As he waits for Puck, Oberon sees Demetrius being pursued by Helena. Thinking to be helpful, Oberon instructs Puck to use the same herb on the eyes of the 'disdainful youth' (2.1.261).

Meanwhile, Lysander and Hermia lie down to sleep in the grove where Titania rests. Puck, thinking that he recognises the young man by his Athenian clothes, puts magic drops in Lysander's eyes. Demetrius rushes through the grove chased by Helena. She is too exhausted to follow. When she sees Lysander she checks if he's dead – he wakes up and falls instantly in love with her. Helena feels mocked and runs away, then Lysander abandons Hermia to follow Helena. Hermia wakes alone after a terrifying dream and runs to find Lysander.

Act 3

In the grove where Titania sleeps, the six Mechanicals meet as planned and try to solve staging difficulties in their play. Bottom walks 'offstage' into the bushes as directed and is transformed by Puck, who wants to have some fun with these amateur actors. When Bottom is called back 'onstage' by the exasperated director Peter Quince, he's wearing an ass's head and his terrified mates scatter, leaving him alone in the wood. As he sings to give himself courage, Titania wakes up, hears his 'beautiful' voice and falls in love with him, calling on her fairies to serve him.

Puck reports Titania's 'love' for a monster to Oberon and confirms he's followed his master's instructions about dosing the Athenian youth. It's the wrong youth, as they discover when Demetrius and Hermia run in, quarrelling. Demetrius falls down exhausted and Puck is sent off to find Helena. Oberon thinks he'll put things right by dosing Demetrius but it only complicates the mistake: when Helena comes in pursued by Lysander both men desire her and start to quarrel. Helena thinks it's a cruel joke, which seems to be confirmed when Hermia comes in and is apparently rejected by Lysander. All four lovers are in a state of confusion, wanting to fight each other, while Puck enjoys the chaos. Oberon will sort things out before morning but tells Puck to keep the young people separated in the wood and use another herb to restore Lysander's love for Hermia. Then he will lift the charm from Titania and 'all things shall be peace' (3.2.377).

Act 4

When Titania and Bottom fall asleep together, Oberon removes the charm from her eyes and Puck restores Bottom's human head. Oberon and Titania are reunited with music and dancing.

At daybreak, Theseus and Hippolyta are out hunting and find the two pairs of young lovers sleeping on the ground. Egeus fumes to see Hermia with Lysander, but Theseus decrees that the couples will be married with him. The royal party returns to Athens. Bottom wakes up and marvels at his 'dream', which must be immortalised in verse by Peter Quince.

Meanwhile, in Athens, Bottom's friends grieve for him and express regret that their play can't go ahead, partly because they would have been well paid. Their mood changes to relief and excitement when Bottom returns with news that their play has been selected.

Act 5

In the palace, the three pairs of newlyweds prepare for an evening's entertainment before bedtime. While Hippolyta muses on the strangeness of the young lovers' stories, Theseus reacts as a rational man dealing with imagination: for him it's all a kind of creative madness, not to be mistaken for reality. The inept performance of 'Pyramus and Thisbe' tries their courtly good manners.

Bottom and his friends conclude with a dance and leave the palace; the lovers go to their marriage beds. Puck returns to sweep the room for Oberon and Titania to sing and dance and bless the couples. Puck concludes the play by speaking directly to the audience and begging for applause.

Character summaries

There are four sets of characters in *A Midsummer Night's Dream*, each of which has its own dramatic significance and development.

In this discussion, and throughout the remainder of this guide, acts and scenes are referred to in an abbreviated form. For example, Act 1, Scene 2 is referred to as 1.2.

1. The court group

These characters do not interact with the fairy world and are preoccupied with their own lives. The last scene in the play lets the fairy world enter the palace.

Theseus is the Duke of Athens, and he rules the city state as chief lawgiver. He is a mature, confident leader in a male-dominated society. In 1.1 he is preparing to marry a foreign warrior woman he's defeated in battle. He appears again in 4.1, when he aims to impress Hippolyta with his hunting dogs. After the Mechanicals' play he thanks them generously, decrees it's bedtime at last for the newlyweds and promises another fortnight of revels to come.

Hippolyta, Queen of the Amazons, is the leader of a tribe of strong fighting women defeated by Theseus. In the hunting scene (4.1) she matches Theseus in a game of classical name-dropping over the hunting dogs, hearing music in their cries. In the final scene of the play, she intuits that there is something more to the strange events the young lovers have described rather than accepting Theseus' attempt to explain them rationally.

Philostrate is the master of the entertainments (revels) at court. His name means 'lover of battles'; he is authorised by Theseus to organise shows for the royal marriage. He appears again in the last scene to advise Theseus on the shows being offered and snobbishly tries to dissuade him from choosing the Mechanicals' play.

The Master of the Revels was an important administrative job in Shakespeare's time and could make or break a new play. Queen

Elizabeth's Master, Sir Edmund Tilney, had the authority to censor or even close down shows and imprison actors.

Egeus is an Athenian gentleman and authoritarian father to Hermia. He tries to prevent his daughter from marrying Lysander. He is finally overruled by Theseus, who permits the marriage. He is not present at the wedding celebrations in the last scene.

2. The lovers

These four young Athenians do not see the fairy world but are manipulated secretly by Oberon and Puck.

Hermia is daughter to Egeus and in love with Lysander, with whom she elopes to avoid marriage to Demetrius. When the lovers come to the wood, Demetrius has followed them and she has to fend off both young men. After waking from a nightmare, Hermia endures the further terror of being abandoned and rejected by Lysander. Puck's magic reunites Hermia and Lysander, and Theseus and Hippolyta find the couple lying together in the wood.

Lysander is in love with Hermia. In 1.1 he criticises Demetrius for being an inconstant lover but then experiences what inconstancy feels like when Puck's mistake with the love juice in 2.2 changes his love object from Hermia to Helena. In the wood with Demetrius, he pursues Helena and the violence simmering in both men is prevented by Puck. Lysander is given the antidote to his love spell by Puck and reunites with Hermia for their wedding at the end of the play.

Demetrius appears very self-assured in the first scene because he is Hermia's father's preferred suitor. Previously 'betrothed' to Helena (4.1.169), he has become obsessed with Hermia and in 2.1 he follows her into the wood, pursued by Helena. Demetrius is sadistic in his speech to drive Helena away, but in 3.2 he is given a dose of love juice by Oberon and when he wakes up he desires Helena again. In 4.1 Demetrius is found sleeping beside Helena and they are finally married happily.

Because she has been humiliated by Demetrius, **Helena** has lost confidence and is consumed with jealousy of her friend Hermia, whom she envies for her happiness with Lysander. In 1.1, she speaks about the transformative power of love but also about blind Cupid's random and treacherous gifts. She betrays her friends by telling Demetrius about their plan, so that she can follow him into the wood. When Lysander suddenly declares his love for her in 2.2, she feels cruelly mocked. In 3.2 she is pursued by both young men; she is almost driven mad because she can only think it's a mocking game – even her best friend Hermia seems to be part of it. However, Helena runs away rather than fight with Hermia. In 4.1 she is found sleeping beside Demetrius and they are paired happily.

3. The Mechanicals

These six Elizabethan 'Athenian' working men are affected by magic in the wood, and one of them, Bottom, is transported into the fairy world and an encounter with the Fairy Queen. For his comedians, Shakespeare chose everyday trades that he might have seen around him in the theatre world – people who could construct stage props and costumes and keep essential things in good working order.

Peter Quince is a carpenter who has written the script of 'Pyramus and Thisbe'. He assigns parts, sets up and directs the group's rehearsal, and decides on costumes and props. Quince delivers the prologue in the performance, but is so overcome with performance nerves that he botches his reading.

We might see Shakespeare playfully including himself in this group of amateurs through the character of Quince, whose name probably derives from *quoins*, the cornerstone, rather than the hard knobbly fruit. Maybe Shakespeare is having a further joke, because Quince does turn to jelly in performance.

Nick Bottom is a weaver who plays Pyramus. He is a confident performer but thinks he's a better actor than he actually is. Puck enchants him, giving him both the head of an ass and the chance to meet the Fairy

Queen. He is the natural and well-liked leader of the Mechanicals, who grieve when they think he must be dead. The group welcomes him back enthusiastically in 4.2, after Puck has restored his human form. Bottom recalls his experience as a wonderful 'dream', then goes on to perform Pyramus with dramatic flair.

Bottom's name makes us laugh, suggesting he's already an 'ass' (a supposedly foolish animal with big ears *and* a rear end) even before he's bewitched, but there's more to him than just being a 'tender ass' (4.1.23). Asses are traditionally associated with wisdom, too, and holiness. More importantly, in weaving, a bottom is a smooth wooden boat-shaped spool holder that slides the spool of weft thread through the warp threads on a loom. A weaver's 'bottom' is therefore an important tool of the trade.

Francis Flute is a bellows-mender who plays Thisbe, tentatively at first but then sometimes stealing the show with the authentic way he delivers Thisbe's lament over Pyramus before Thisbe kills herself for love. His surname describes the tube at the end of a pair of bellows, through which air is blown. Everybody in Shakespeare's time would have these useful objects, simply constructed with two flat pieces of wood with handles, joined by leather hinges and holding a leather bag. The mender would be in constant demand as hinges and bags were always wearing out.

Tom Snout is a tinker, or tinsmith, who plays Wall. He would need to know how to build a small furnace with walls of roughcast (plaster mixed with stones) to work the metal. He's practical but literal-minded, scoffing at the idea of bringing a wall indoors before appealing to Bottom for the solution in 3.1.

Snug, who plays Lion, is a joiner – someone who joins wooden shapes to make frames, steps and other basic furniture pieces. Quince the carpenter then does the major construction and finishing. Snug is timid and slow of study.

Robin Starveling is a tailor who plays Moonshine by personifying the moon with traditional props showing he's the Man in the Moon: a dog, a thornbush and a lantern. This was a well-known ancient story of a man banished to the moon for collecting firewood on the Sabbath (traditionally a day of rest). An ordinary tailor might be poor and ill-fed, as Starveling's name suggests, but a costume maker for a court masque could make a fortune.

4. The fairies

The fairies are invisible to mortals and have specific tasks in the natural world.

Oberon, the King of the Fairies, has power over both the natural and the supernatural worlds. His exotic appearance and volatile temperament are on show in 2.1, when he and Titania meet by moonlight in the wood outside Athens and argue bitterly over a changeling child they both want but won't share. Angered by Titania's refusal to submit to his wishes, Oberon devises a way to punish her with a humiliating spell. He sends his servant Puck to get a special flower, whose magic love juice he will drop into Titania's eyes so that she will become besotted with some wild creature. He also starts to interfere in the conflicts between the human couples he sees running through the wood. In 4.1, after releasing Titania from her deluded obsession with Bottom, Oberon makes peace with his beloved queen and they dance together. At the close of the play, he leads the fairy dance around the sleeping palace to bless the married couples and their offspring.

Titania is the Fairy Queen. Her name suggests she's the daughter of Titans, a mythical race of giants, although the joke is she is much smaller, like the tiny fairies she commands. In 2.1 she points out how destructive the quarrel with Oberon is to the natural world they influence, but she refuses to give up the Indian child she is rearing in memory of a mortal woman who was her follower and friend. When Titania sleeps, Oberon drops the love juice in her eyes and she wakes to hear a transformed Bottom singing. Immediately she is enthralled with her new lover and has her fairies carry him off to her bower, where she cuddles Bottom to sleep. Once Oberon removes the spell, Titania happily takes her husband's hand to dance, as she does again in the palace at the end of the play.

Also known by his folklore name Robin Goodfellow, **Puck** is the lively servant of Oberon, with whom he has a close bond. Shakespeare's original audience knew him well as a trickster hobgoblin (an earth demon) from folklore, identified with domestic tasks and love pranks. He has a dark side, expressed in his association with frightening night creatures, ghosts and the occult. He is very acrobatic, zooming around the stage on errands for Oberon. He is independent to a degree and selects Bottom as his personal victim to enchant.

Cobweb is one of Titania's four named fairies who attend on Bottom. Cobweb's name calls to mind the delicacy of a cobweb but also its folk-medicinal value in Shakespeare's time, when cobwebs were used to wrap and heal cuts.

Peaseblossom's name derives from the pea family, which was a staple food of ordinary people. A common saying was 'Peascod time is wooing time', hence Bottom's naughty joke about little Peaseblossom's parents, Mistress Squash and Master Peascod (3.1.164–5), ripe and full of peas ('cods' are testicles, as in a 'codpiece').

Mustardseed is a tiny but strong fairy, whose name also has medicinal associations; a mustard poultice or plaster was applied to ease muscular aches and pains with its penetrating heat. Mustard seeds were also ground up with vinegar and water to make the traditional hot sauce for roast beef.

Moth is a little winged night fairy; for Elizabethans her name would have called to mind a folk remedy made of summer moths steeped in rose petals to treat kidney problems.

BACKGROUND & CONTEXT

The title

Midsummer Night, St. John's Eve and the Summer Solstice (a holiday time celebrated around 20–24 June in the northern hemisphere) traditionally has significance in Europe, where people still welcome the sunrise at Stonehenge, make bonfires, feast, dance around maypoles and gather medicinal herbs by moonlight to ward off evil spirits and promote love. Ripening crops and water bathed in moonlight are blessed, and babies are considered especially lucky to be baptised on John the Baptist's birthday, celebrated on 24 June.

You can see how Shakespeare played with these ideas in *A Midsummer Night's Dream*: it was a celebration of sexual expression and community goodwill. It was also a powerfully magical time, being the night when everyday human life could encounter the supernatural. Peter Quince tells his actors to meet for rehearsals at the Duke's oak in the wood (1.2.87). The ancient Celtic name for the oak tree is 'duir', meaning 'door': the oak is a doorway between worlds, a well-known site for fairy abductions of mortals in popular stories. Puck says that Titania's bower is nearby (3.2.7–12).

Dreams mix up what we desire, fear and hope for in a surreal imaginative combination that is beyond conscious rational control. Shakespeare mixes together all the aspects of midsummer revels to create a collective 'dream' experience for audience and characters alike.

Shakespeare's theatrical context

Theatre was a relatively new form of public entertainment in Elizabethan England and professional acting was a very new profession, dependent on titled patrons for support. They enjoyed the prestige of owning a company of players named for them, like owning a major football club today. Shakespeare was born at just the right time to take advantage of this surge of excitement about theatre.

Shakespeare was twelve when the first purpose-built theatre to house the Earl of Leicester's Men opened in London in 1576. You can tell how new the whole idea was by the very name of the venue, just called 'The Theatre' by its builder, actor and manager James Burbage. It was followed by others with fancier names like The Curtain (1577), then The Rose (1587) and The Swan (1595). We associate Shakespeare most of all with The Globe, a theatre built in 1599 on Bankside (on the south side of the River Thames) to house the Lord Chamberlain's Men, but his plays were being staged and became popular at the older playhouses. In his 1590s play *Henry V*, for example, the circular open-air auditorium described at the start by Chorus as 'this wooden O' could as easily have been The Theatre or The Curtain as The Globe.

Because theatres in Shakespeare's time were constructed on a roughly circular plan, audiences could sit or stand on three sides of a thrust stage. There would be bench seating on the ground floor and two upper floors for two pennies or threepence with a cushion, plus more expensive private gentlemen's and lords' rooms with comfortable views of the stage – where they could see and be seen. The open yard area closest to the stage was for the 'groundlings' who paid one penny and stood to watch the show. All kinds of people came to the plays, including local Londoners and foreign visitors, men and women, as long as they could afford to pay their pennies into the box at the door – the box office.

Actors learned how to play to the crowd: some actors at the London Globe now report that it feels like being at a rock concert or football match. The original Globe audience could be well over three thousand people and its contemporary reincarnation in London has a full house of over fifteen hundred patrons, all very close to the action.

Theatre floor plans meant that an interplay was possible between actors and audience members. Shakespeare understood this very well. Actors could direct words to particular parts of the crowd, for example, or catch the eye of a single individual. If an actor wanted his character to step out of the play's world to talk to the audience, he could do that easily, as Puck demonstrates when he wishes the audience goodnight.

Shakespeare wrote important soliloquies in his plays – solo speeches in which a character can reveal their innermost thoughts, and which the audience learned to understand was for their ears only. In *A Midsummer Night's Dream*, for example, Helena delivers her soliloquy about love, beginning 'How happy some o'er other some can be', when she's left alone onstage at the end of 1.1. Later, Bottom wakes alone from his dream to give his puzzled yet joyous soliloquy at the end of 4.1.

Plays were performed in full daylight, with few props and no fixed scenery, and the audience's attention would be focused on costumed players performing on an elevated platform thrust out from a back wall. This wall usually had two entrance/exit doors to a 'tiring room' (a dressing room and props area). There would also be a central curtained 'inner room' or 'discovery space' in the wall, with a balcony on the floor level above and usually a place for a few musicians at the side or on the top level. The stage area was big: imagine the size of a tennis court from baseline to net.

Notice how creatively Shakespeare writes scenes for this space in *A Midsummer Night's Dream*. In Act 2, Oberon and Puck observe the lovers chasing around, then Titania falls asleep nearby, and then at the start of Act 3 the Mechanicals enter to set up their rehearsal. In Act 5, the onstage courtly audience members comment while enjoying 'Pyramus and Thisbe' – and the theatre audience watches them all.

In Shakespeare's time, all stage performers had to be male. Women were forbidden by law from performing; noble ladies could take part in masques at court, and foreign troupes with women occasionally played, but these were the rare exceptions. Teenage boys were trained to act convincingly in women's roles. *A Midsummer Night's Dream* required experienced boy actors for Hippolyta and Titania (possibly doubled by one good player), two more for Hermia and Helena, and another young man in the character of Flute taking on a deliberately exaggerated 'girly' parody as Thisbe.

GENRE, STRUCTURE & LANGUAGE

Genre

A Midsummer Night's Dream is a **comedy** harking back to classical Greek forms and character types – with mistakes, problems, puzzles and family disagreements. All ends well, with paired couples and a wedding celebration. Shakespeare enriches his comic material in several ways.

- He includes 'Pyramus and Thisbe', a play-within-the-play, which pushes comedy into a **burlesque** on a tragic love story; in a burlesque, a serious subject is treated comically, to exaggerate and mock qualities in an overly pretentious original. Shakespeare knew Ovid's story of the tragic lovers in Golding's flowery, moralised translation of *Metamorphoses* (1567).
- He layers classical mythology with folk and fairy lore, drawing on a fashion for magic scenarios with lyrical fairies in the 1580s and 1590s. Puck, aka Robin Goodfellow, sweeps the palace floor with a broom in a familiar folk-play gesture to clear 'dramatic space', before fairies sing and dance in the palace to end the play.
- He incorporates material from popular pamphlet literature about Robin Goodfellow plus Reginald Scot's *The Discoverie of Witchcraft* (1584), which described Puck and magic spells in ointments that could make a man look as though he had the head of an ass.

Structure

A Midsummer Night's Dream has nine scenes, spread over five acts. The action takes place over several nights and in two locations, Athens and an enchanted wood near the city.

As is typical in a comedy, **Act 1** is the **exposition**, an introduction to main characters, the setting, the play's main concerns and some of its complications. **Act 2** is the **rising action** where complications and conflicts are intensified. **Act 3** reaches a **climax**, the maximum point of trouble. **Act 4** moves towards **resolution**, then **Act 5** ends with **celebration** and **marriage**.

The two contrasting settings represent different ways of experiencing social relationships. Athens is an urban place of **Apollonian** reason, law and order, uniting Elizabethan London and Greek mythic time. The wood outside the town is traditionally a **Dionysian** place for physical and emotional freedom, as well as potentially dangerous mayhem. Apollo and Dionysus are Greek gods associated with the very beginning of classical theatre. Find out more about them and their attributes, because they represent contrary states of mental experience and expression explored in *A Midsummer Night's Dream*.

Language

Shakespeare manipulates language to create different moods, using contrasting rhythms, verse forms and prose. Analysing the verse structures helps you attune your ears to subtle shifts in language patterns that reflect changing dynamics and feelings between the characters.

Iambic pentameter and blank verse (x / x / x / x / x /)

This rhythmic pattern consists of five unstressed/stressed pairs in a line. Its rhythm is like a heartbeat and it is the underlying pulse of spoken English. Blank verse, or unrhymed iambic pentameter, is the most common form of dialogue in Shakespeare's plays. Shakespeare perfected this type of verse: it works for formal interactions, expressing nuances from loving seriousness to cold politeness to violent disagreement. Shakespeare's iambic pentameter isn't mathematically rigid, so expect occasional extra syllables, variations in stress patterns or tensions in the rhythms. Here is an example:

> Here **come** the **lov**ers, **full** of **joy** and **mirth**. (Theseus, 5.1.28)

Rhyming verse

This is usually written as couplets, with the end words of two consecutive lines rhyming. The young lovers often speak in rhyming couplets. For example:

> By all the vows that ever men have **broke** –
> (In number more than ever women **spoke**) …
> (Hermia, 1.1.175–6)

Rhyming verse is also used for the fairies and the Mechanicals (in their old-fashioned recitation of lines for 'Pyramus and Thisbe').

Trochaic tetrameter or 'fairy speech' (/ x / x / x / x)

This metre has four stressed/unstressed pairs in a line, sometimes missing the last beat, as in Oberon's chanted spell:

> **What** thou **seest** when **thou** dost **wake**,
> **Do** it **for** thy **true** love **take** … (Oberon, 2.2.33–4)

Prose

Prose is used for everyday speech; it is conversational, with no set rhythm or poetic structure. In Shakespearean drama, prose is mostly but not exclusively used by 'ordinary people'. The Mechanicals' dialogue is written as prose (unless they're reciting their play lines in verse), and it is also used for Bottom's dialogue with the fairies.

Music

A Midsummer Night's Dream has inspired wonderful music by famous composers, even though no original music survives from Shakespeare's own staging. His playhouse band of musicians would have performed on cue for the fairies' lullaby in 2.2, and then for dancing as spells are lifted in 4.1 and again in 5.1 when the fairies dance through the palace. Musicians may have played to make the 'rough music' for Bottom's tongs and bones and sounded hunting horns to wake the lovers in 4.1.

SCENE-BY-SCENE ANALYSIS

Act 1

1.1 Summary: *(Athens, Theseus' palace) The play opens with Theseus and Hippolyta looking at the waning moon. Egeus interrupts with his complaint against his daughter for disobedience. Lysander and Hermia tell Helena their plan to elope through the wood the following night.*

The royal couple, Duke Theseus and his wife-to-be Queen Hippolyta, anticipate their marriage in four days' time but the mood is not as happy as you might expect. How do we get the feeling that they're not exactly 'over the moon' with joy?

Key point

Look out for moon imagery throughout the play – from the first scene it underpins different attitudes to love, sexuality and change. Since ancient times the moon has been worshipped as the great triple goddess Hecate, representing three female life stages. The virgin huntress, called Diana (Roman) or Artemis (Greek), is represented by the new moon. Luna (Roman) or Selene (Greek) is the maternal full moon. Hecate is the pale-faced old woman (or wise Crone) of the waning dark moon. Shakespeare uses all these names in the play. The great goddess in her various manifestations was well known to Elizabethans, as a powerful and paradoxical symbol of magic, witchcraft, medicinal herbs, transitional states of being, entrances to other worlds, madness (note the connection to the moon in the word 'lunacy'), dreams, ghosts, love and night.

Theseus may sound polite and courtly but he's impatient. His negative characterisation of the old waning moon as a stepmother or a rich old widow holding back his inheritance by not dying fast enough links material possession with sexual desire and obstinate femaleness. He continues with negative images of 'the pale companion' (Hecate, l.15) getting in the way of marriage celebrations, and later he urges Hermia to reject the life of 'a barren sister' (l.72) and 'the cold fruitless moon' (l.73).

Q How do we know that Theseus also notices how the conversation has upset Hippolyta, though she has remained silent?

Egeus attacks Lysander for using the moon's supernatural powers to enchant Hermia, asserting that Lysander has bewitched her with poetry and sung love songs to her in the moonlight.

This opening scene is important because it sets the tone of the play to come, alerting us to look out for difficulties between lovers as they negotiate relationships. Later in the scene Lysander notes that every love story he's heard points to the sad reality that 'the course of true love never did run smooth' (l.134).

Left alone, Lysander and Hermia show how absorbed they are in each other in the repetitive shared pattern of their lamenting dialogue about doomed love, which connects shadows and dreams. This begins the play's dream imagery, which will be extended to all characters.

When Lysander proposes that they elope, we notice that his idea of a dowager, his kind and helpful old aunt, is in sharp contrast to the image Theseus created. Hermia's solemn vow demonstrates the strength of a woman's love (even if men are false), and she cites the unfortunate Queen Dido of Carthage as an example. Everyone in Shakespeare's audience would have recognised Dido as a classical example of faithful love: when abandoned by her lover Aeneas and feeling herself dishonoured, she built her funeral pyre, stabbed herself and fell into the flames. Her 'false' lover, the Trojan hero Aeneas, deserted her to fulfil another destiny. Not all love ends well.

At this moment, Helena, the girlfriend Demetrius jilted, arrives. The girls, who have been close friends, exchange quick single lines of dialogue (called *stichomythia*) which winds up the emotional tension between them. Hermia and Lysander try to comfort Helena by revealing their plan to leave Athens. Helena sees an opportunity to tell Demetrius and, if only briefly, gain his attention and thanks.

Q What do you think Hippolyta the Amazon Queen might be thinking about? She stays silent in this scene.

1.2 Summary: *(Athens, in the town) The Mechanicals plan their contribution to the entertainments they've heard about and agree to rehearse their Interlude the next evening in the wood.*

The dramatic mood changes as six tradies (the Mechanicals), speaking in prose, assemble to discuss plans for their Interlude. This and the next rehearsal scene (3.1) are full of information about how plays were set up and cast in Shakespeare's time.

Bottom has a habit of mispronouncing and confusing words, evident in **malapropisms** such as 'aggravate' for 'modulate' (l.66) and 'obscenely' for 'discreetly' (l.85). A malapropism is a verbal blunder in which a word with a similar sound but very different meaning is substituted for the intended word. The name is derived from the later stage character, Mrs Malaprop ('Mrs inappropriate') in Richard Sheridan's 1775 play *The Rivals*. Shakespeare was already using the verbal fumble for comic effect in his plays long before Sheridan.

Shakespeare has fun with Bottom wanting to play every role, demonstrating his acting range with different voices and ranting speeches. And 'Thisbe' will be played by Flute, despite his objections and preference for playing a romantic hero like a 'wandering knight' (l.37).

Q How does this scene help us think about the idea of transformation by contrasting literal-mindedness with the imaginative 'suspension of disbelief'?

Act 2

2.1 Summary: *(The wood) Puck meets one of Titania's fairies in the wood, then Oberon and Titania meet and argue. Demetrius, pursued by Helena, comes to the wood in search of Lysander and Hermia. Oberon sends Puck to find a flower for the love charm.*

The action moves to the wood on the night of the following day and introduces the fairy world, which has its own serious disturbances. The interaction between Puck and the fairy tells the audience what each of them does and explains why their master and mistress are quarrelling.

It's another example of a couple in conflict, made more dangerous because King Oberon and Queen Titania are powerful elemental spirits. Their actions have disturbing consequences for the natural and human worlds, as Titania explains in her impassioned speech (l.88–117). Some commentators note that the 1590s were years of bad weather conditions, failing harvests and extreme hardship in England – all of which Titania describes.

The source of their marital conflict harks back to Theseus (whom Titania loves – she has helped him to seduce several women before Hippolyta) and Oberon's 'warrior love' (l.71), the 'bouncing Amazon' (l.70) Hippolyta in her hunting boots. They spit out accusations to each other, revealing their resentment and sexual jealousy.

This scene raises questions of a double standard in sexual freedoms that you could discuss – men (especially heroes like Theseus) assume their actions have no repercussions, while women are used and abandoned. Look up the classical names Perigenia (also spelled Perigouna or Perigune), Aegles (also spelled Aegle) and especially Ariadne, who helped Theseus kill the Minotaur in the Cretan labyrinth. Their stories are all in one of Shakespeare's sources, Plutarch's *Lives*.

Key point

Titania leaves after refusing to submit to her husband's demand for the changeling she is protecting to honour the boy's dead mother. In Shakespeare's time, fairies were sometimes believed to exchange one of their own sickly babies for a healthy human one, but Titania has simply taken this child, leaving no substitute. With minimal medical understanding of illness and genetic differences, especially those related to birth 'defects' (like moles, harelips and scars, referenced by Oberon at 5.1.389), unhealthy or otherwise imperfect babies were sometimes spoken of unkindly as 'changelings', to explain away the natural reality. Look ahead to Oberon's specific defensive blessings on the offspring of the newly married couples at the end of Act 5 to underline the significance of this social belief.

Oberon has two key speeches in the scene.

- In lines 148–74, he reflects on how 'love-in-idleness' (l.168) came into being accidently through Cupid's misfired love arrow. He includes a direct compliment to the 'fair vestal thronèd by the west' (l.158), i.e. Queen Elizabeth I, whose goddess-like virtue was supernaturally protected by 'chaste' moonbeams (l.162), even though the incident directly caused a powerful love charm to be created. Ironically, Oberon intends to use love as a malicious weapon against Titania.

- In lines 249–66, while Puck rushes away to find the flower, Oberon contemplates what wild beast Titania will see after her eyes have been anointed with the love juice. His seductively beautiful description of Titania's flowery bed, beginning 'I know a bank' (l.249), turns sour as his cruel intention to 'make her full of hateful fantasies' (l.258) is revealed.

The conversation between Oberon and Puck is interrupted by a fierce argument between two humans, as Demetrius is pursued by the lovesick Helena. They resort to various kinds of word play, echoing each other's lines and reversing ideas, with metaphors to express their frustration. Demetrius starts with a pun, feeling 'wood' (going mad) 'within this wood' (l.192). Helena responds with an exaggerated metaphor called a conceit, calling him the 'adamant' (l.195, by which she means a hard diamond, or sometimes metal, with magnetic properties), which draws her heart 'true as steel' (l.197) towards him. Changing her imagery, she identifies herself as his 'spaniel' (l.203), who would welcome ill-treatment rather than no attention at all. Demetrius nastily hints at sexual 'mischief in the wood' (l.237).

Oberon observes the quarrel and is motivated to help Helena reclaim her errant lover. Perhaps he sees something in her situation with Demetrius that causes him to reflect on his own relationship with Titania.

Q Oberon/Theseus and Titania/Hippolyta are often doubled by the same actors in productions. How can doubling give us a glimpse of the 'alter ego' of each character?

Q Find out about the classical myth of Apollo and Daphne, which Helena references in lines 230–4. How does Helena rework and reverse this myth to describe her own situation?

Q Oberon thinks his instructions to Puck about identifying the Athenian lover are specific enough. Why aren't they?

2.2 Summary: *(The wood) Titania goes to sleep in a grove, and Oberon anoints her eyes with the love charm. Lysander and Hermia arrive in same grove exhausted and lie down to sleep. Puck thinks that Lysander is the 'Athenian' to enchant, and puts the juice on his eyes. Helena enters the grove, still following Demetrius, so when Lysander wakes and sees her he falls in love with her. Lysander pursues Helena, then Hermia wakes from a 'snake' nightmare and finds she's left alone.*

The fairy world and the lovers' disordered perceptions draw closer together in this scene, as the love juice creates further confusion.

Look carefully at the words of the fairies' lullaby for the Fairy Queen (l.9–30), which is intended to set a restful mood and work a protective charm around Titania. Contrast the fairies' words and song rhythms with Oberon's forceful trochaic couplets (see page 16) as he anoints Titania's eyes and delivers the incantation that she will 'wake when some vile thing is near' (l.40).

Shakespeare's audience would have registered an ambiguous significance in the idea of Philomel (the nightingale, l.13) singing beautifully to Titania, because what changed the mythical Philomel from woman to bird in Ovid's story was rape and mutilation. Even a trace of that memory in people's minds unsettles the moment when Titania falls asleep and becomes vulnerable to Oberon's invasion of her bower.

Key point

Sexual tension of a gentler kind underpins the next part of the scene as Lysander and Hermia, lost in the wood and tired out, settle down to sleep. Notice that they speak in rhyming couplets, lovers' talk, and share an affectionate pun about 'lying' together (l.57–61). Hermia modestly appeals to his 'courtesy' as 'a virtuous bachelor' (l.62, l.65) and they lie down separately ... which causes Puck to misinterpret chastity as lack of affection and mistake the identity of the youth he is to dose with the love charm.

Shared rhyming couplets underline the division between Demetrius and Helena as he rushes away. She has another important short speech about being ugly and unloved, before a sudden comic reversal as she stumbles over Lysander, who wakes up and immediately declares himself in love with her. He follows her under the romantic delusion that he can somehow be Helena's 'knight' (l.150). Remember Flute's romantic aspiration to be cast as a 'wandering knight', too (1.2.37).

Q How does Hermia's nightmare, in which Lysander watches on, 'smiling', as her heart is eaten by a snake (l.155–6), foreshadow (predict) what she experiences in 3.2?

Act 3

3.1 Summary: *(The wood) Quince and the actors come to the wood to rehearse as planned. Puck enchants Bottom, giving him an ass's head. Titania wakes and instantly falls in love with Bottom.*

This is a key scene where Shakespeare is playing with the idea of illusion in several ways: theatrical, visual, aural and perceptual.

Theatrical illusion

Quince has to explain the idea of dialogue – that you must listen and wait for cues, and pick up lines quickly to make conversations sound spontaneous. (The actors get individual parts with cues rather than full scripts, which contributes further to their insecurity.) It's about anxious amateurs in early theatre wrestling with the power of visual illusion, too. How can you make moonshine happen? Solution: Starveling can *personify* the composite idea of Moonshine as the Man in the Moon, with lantern, thornbush and dog (you can research the origins of this story). In a similar way, Snout can *personify* 'Wall' with a costume and an identifying speech.

Bottom's solution to a perceived problem of onstage killing is to 'explain' theatrical illusion in a special prologue – the kind of thing that wrecks the very emotional engagement an audience expects and actors work for, called the 'suspension of disbelief'. The same issue applies to 'Lion', who is told he must speak out as Snug to quell audience fears of an actual wild beast.

As Bottom insists on explaining away illusion, he's making himself more *real* to an audience, and so adding to the success of the illusion. Everything he says enhances the appeal of his comic foolishness for an audience.

Key point

The 'alienation effect' was a deliberate performance strategy used by twentieth-century German dramatist Bertolt Brecht to make audiences look more thoughtfully at what they were seeing onstage. Brecht insisted that his audiences did not simply accept the theatrical illusion or story by suspending disbelief, but looked through the illusion at the political meaning behind the story. So his performers sometimes 'step out of character' to startle the audience to a new way of engaging with, questioning and understanding a play. Shakespeare uses a similar technique in direct address to the audience, with asides and soliloquies that encourage the audience to think as well as be entertained.

Aural and visual illusions

When Quince and the other Mechanicals scatter in panic, Puck chases them and scares them with sounds and images, making wild animal cries and raising will-o'-the-wisp fire (flickers of marsh gas, thought to be ghostly and given to leading travellers astray from a safe path at night). Comedy is edging into a darker side of uncertainty and terror, familiar to early audiences from writings about Puck's ambiguous mischief-making in Reginald Scot's *The Discoverie of Witchcraft* (1584), a book Shakespeare knew. Paradoxically, disturbing fears can be generated by Puck's ideas of having fun.

Perceptual illusions

Bottom underlines the idea that 'reason and love keep little company together nowadays' (l.120–1). Left alone in the wood, he is terrified but tries to stay brave by singing (including 'nays' and donkey braying sounds). Titania, under the love spell's illusion, is woken by Bottom's absurd 'angel' voice (l.107) and smitten by what she sees.

Note Titania's strange speech (l.175–7) as fairies carry Bottom to her bower. What is she describing? If dew is the moon's way of weeping for violated chastity, whose chastity is it? Perhaps Bottom's, about to be lost? Is Bottom about to be changed sexually by his encounter with the Fairy Queen?

Q The 'rehearsal' discussion is **metatheatrical** – about what theatre is – and very funny, as anyone involved in putting on a show knows. Do you think this scene helps us understand more about what theatre really is? Explain your answer.

Q How does Bottom respond to Titania's sexual advances? When he wants to find a way out of the wood, she forcibly forbids him to leave. Is he Titania's captive, as Hippolyta is to Theseus? Do we feel some sympathy for Bottom, especially as he's not fully aware of what's happening to him?

3.2 Summary: *(The wood) Puck and Oberon observe the lovers' painful confusion. Oberon will intervene and, with Puck's help, make all well by daybreak.*

This scene needs a lot of careful choreography to work smoothly onstage for maximum visual comedy *and* to bring out the underlying disharmony that could cause irreparable harm to the lovers' relationships, even leading to physical harm if the men are allowed to fight. Pay close attention to the way language patterns shift to indicate changing relationships between the young lovers.

As a comic prelude to the human quarrel scene, note Puck's delighted report to Oberon of the mayhem he's caused for Titania with Bottom the monster, together with his pride in having remedied the young lovers' problem as instructed. His satisfaction is undercut immediately when Hermia arrives and accuses Demetrius of murdering Lysander. Puck has made a mistake. This is a good example of **dramatic irony**, which occurs when the audience knows something important that the characters don't yet know. In this case, we know – but the lovers don't know – that Puck has interfered and his incompetence has made the situation worse. What will happen when they find out? Oberon's opening question is another example of something *we* already know the answer to.

Key point

Oberon drops the love juice into Demetrius' eyes to restore his love for Helena, but fairy magic is thwarted as Lysander and Helena's argument wakes Demetrius too soon. Puck may think it delightful 'sport … those things do best please me / That befall prepost'rously' (l.119–21), but it shifts the dramatic mood into a much more serious kind of comic confusion. This is signalled by the way Lysander and Helena speak to each other in a closely rhymed emotional exchange, similar to a shared love sonnet (l.122–35), even though the feelings expressed are not mutual.

Although both young men change affections (under the illusion of the love spell), the two women never waver in their love for their original partners. Why are Hermia and Helena so ready to accept as truthful what their changed men say? Do either of them try to keep a grasp on reality, as they understand it, to avert a fight?

Hermia and Helena turn on each other as their rhymed couplet speech patterns turn into more formal verse when Helena accuses 'injurious Hermia' (l.195) of betraying sisterly friendship; whereas they had done things together as one, they are now divided into two. Their insults hurt because they target things people can't change about themselves, such as physical characteristics and appearance (e.g. 'puppet', l.288; 'painted maypole', l.296; 'dwarf', l.328). They are also laced with racist slurs ('Ethiop', l.257; 'tawny Tartar', l.263) and supposed character deficiencies ('canker-blossom', l.282; 'vixen', l.328).

As the warring lovers all run away from each other in distressed confusion, Oberon's mood changes and we sense the assurance of comic resolution, which he will bring about with more herbal magic and Puck's assistance. Although Puck is thoroughly entertained – 'their jangling I esteem a sport' (l.353) – Oberon wants to restore peace in the human world and recover harmony in his own relationship with Titania – *if* she will give him the changeling boy.

Key point

Oberon as the most powerful supernatural being takes on the role of *deus ex machina*, stepping in to fix seemingly irresolvable disorder. This Latin term literally means 'the god from the machine'; it originates in ancient Greek drama, where a masked god like Apollo 'flies in' above the stage on the arm of a wooden crane [a mechane] to deliver divine instructions about justice and properly ending the play.

The play's mood softens and calms at the end of this scene. There is a sense of being at the edge of dawn, a transition time for fairies who will retreat with the night. Puck's warning about 'damnèd spirits' (l.382) still makes us shudder but is countered by Oberon's positive assertion that they are 'spirits of another sort' (l.388) who can look safely on sunrise over the ocean. Nonetheless, Oberon wants everything sorted out by dawn because tomorrow is Theseus' wedding day:

> When they next wake, all this derision
> Shall seem a dream and fruitless vision,
> And back to Athens shall the lovers wend
> With league whose date till death shall never end. (l.370–3)

Puck counts off the couples ('two of both kinds makes up four', l.438) as they collapse with exhaustion, and he casts over them a chanted spell of coupledom, ending with the formula 'Jack shall have Jill' (l.461). They will conform to heteronormative pairings, which would have been the only socially and legally acceptable marital pairing in Shakespeare's time.

Q Are we encouraged to have any sympathy for the spellbound male lovers? Is it easier to understand how and why the young women get tangled up by confused signals?

Q Is the 'Jack and Jill' solution satisfactory to everyone in the play? In what ways can our feelings and perspectives differ today? Research several contemporary productions that explore other possibilities for individuals in casting and directing choices.

Act 4

4.1 Summary *(The wood) Bottom and Titania sleep together, then Oberon removes the charm from her eyes. The Fairy King and Queen are reconciled and at the next midnight will dance at Theseus' wedding. Puck removes the ass's head from Bottom. Hunting in the early morning, Theseus and Hippolyta find the sleeping pairs of lovers, then they all return to Athens for weddings. Bottom wakes from his 'dream'.*

This scene unfolds in four stages as the play's main themes are restated while discord is gradually resolved.

Bottom has settled into being served in ridiculous ways by Titania's fairies. Compare his crude taste in music, favouring 'the tongs and the bones' (metal tongs struck like a triangle, and bones that make a clacking sound knocked together, l.26–7), with the fairies' delicate poetic songs. He's still the same old Bottom, making malapropisms like an 'exposition' (disposition) of sleep (l.35). The disparity between these 'lovers' is apparent: how they use language exposes the gulf that will forever separate them – her verse, his prose.

Oberon intervenes to restore normality, so that Bottom will 'think no more of this night's accidents / But as the fierce vexation of a dream' (l.65–6). Titania recovers her normal sight and recoils from Bottom before Oberon specifically asks Puck to disenchant the man so that he may see again with his 'own fool's eyes' (l.81).

Oberon summons music and dancing to 'rock the ground' (l.83) for the sleepers, like a cradle – a lovely image that suggests they will wake new born into adult life. He reminds the audience that the coming day's marriages will lead to more dancing, a symbol of being 'new in amity' (l.84).

Then the dreamy mood is dissipated by the noise of Theseus and Hippolyta, hunting in the early morning, accompanied by huntsmen with horns and great hounds barking – a different kind of music altogether, which wakes the sleepers. For Elizabethans, hunting imagery was erotic (and sometimes violent), associated metaphorically with a sexual chase by a hunter pursuing his prey, often imagined as a deer. Hunting *is* courtship for Theseus and Hippolyta.

The young Athenian lovers, left alone, join in a short verbal quartet to share their bemused ideas about reality and dreams. Finally, Bottom wakes up and tries to articulate his 'most rare vision' (l.200). Bottom's dream is a reminder to the audience that the 'dream' is not over yet.

Q Why does Puck have to remind Oberon that dawn has broken?

Q Are Theseus and Hippolyta any closer to being in harmony than they seemed to be in 1.1? What might change things for them in this scene?

4.2 Summary: *(Athens) Bottom is reunited with his friends; their play has been chosen.*

This short but important transitional scene takes the Mechanicals from grief to elation. They think they've lost a friend who was bewitched and missing, presumed dead; this colours all their thoughts, but the audience knows Bottom's on his way back. This is another example of dramatic irony, this time lightening the despondent mood.

The aspiring actors feel disappointment at what seems a lost chance to step outside their everyday lives and be rewarded. Flute expresses the group's feeling in his question to Quince: 'It goes not forward. Doth it?' (l.3–4). That question articulates a last desperate shred of hope.

Flute continues his mourning for Bottom: 'Thus hath he lost sixpence a day during his life' (l.15–16). Sixpence could be a very good daily wage for artisans (like carpenters, joiners and tailors) in 1590, so being granted sixpence a day for life was roughly like getting a day's pay free every day. A professional actor could earn about 6 shillings (72 pence) per week and Shakespeare could earn several pounds for writing a play for his company.

Q What do their reactions before Bottom returns, and then when he appears, tell us about how these mates feel about one another?

Q How realistic is the Mechanicals' view that they have a good show to present if given the chance?

Act 5

5.1 Summary *(Athens, the palace) At night, the Mechanicals perform 'Pyramus and Thisbe' before Theseus and the court. Fairies bless the married pairs of lovers in the house, and Puck concludes the play.*

The last scene unfolds in three interlinked steps. It opens with the court, recapitulating important ideas about strangeness, love, truth, transformation, fantasies, imagination, what a poet [writer] does to give 'things unknown' a shape (l.15), and how reason responds to illusion.

Theseus gives a key speech (l.2–22) in which he tries to explain what 'the lunatic, the lover, and the poet' (l.7) apprehend and comprehend, and how the incomprehensible power of 'imagination bodies forth / The forms of things unknown' (l.14–15). He is not entirely approving of the creative poet who constructs words to give to 'airy nothing / A local habitation and a name' (l.16–17). This is Shakespeare making a reflexive joke by writing a character called 'Theseus', who critiques what the poet has imagined and written about. As the scene progresses, notice how Theseus modifies his attitude.

The strangeness of the lovers' accounts of what happened to them in the wood intrigues Hippolyta, who is less sceptical than Theseus about what they've heard and accepts that minds have been 'transfigured' in the night, amounting to 'something of great constancy' (l.24, l.26).

Key point

Shakespeare often constructs his dramatic ideas around contrasting binary pairs (love/hate, darkness/light etc.) and the subtle play of opposites, like nothing and something. Think about Theseus' dismissive words 'airy nothing', because Shakespeare often explores how loaded an apparently throwaway word like 'nothing' can be. Theseus is challenged to think more carefully when a horrified Philostrate insists that the crude entertainment chosen (the Mechanicals' play) is 'nothing, nothing in the world' (l.78). Intrigued by the paradoxical description of a 'tedious brief scene' of 'very tragical mirth' (l.56–7), Theseus aims to reassure Hippolyta that they must be tolerant of the show: 'The kinder we, to give them thanks for nothing' (l.89), even if the simple actors are hopeless and (as she fears) 'can do nothing in this kind' (l.88).

In the Mechanicals' performance of 'Pyramus and Thisbe', the players demonstrate every error you'd find in an amateur performance. It takes great comic skills to work the laughs, especially when the court audience is constantly interrupting with witty remarks. Who gets the theatre audience's laughs and where are our sympathies?

- The performance begins shakily with Quince's anxious mangling of sensible punctuation ('points' and 'the stop', l.118, l.120) in his prologue. Quince fires up with excitement when he gets to the alliteration (repeated 'b' words) to describe how Pyramus kills himself – usually spraying the words out into the audience with Bottom miming energetically.
- Snout has to explain himself and his (usually rudely positioned) 'chink' (l.156) in his costume as Wall, provoking the better educated Demetrius to make a sharp gag about 'the wittiest partition' (l.164) he's heard (partition as 'wall' and as a section in a formal speech).
- Snug as Lion undercuts the dramatic effect he hopes to create by insisting he's a) not dangerous and b) not even a lion, just in case his audience might be deceived by his appearance.
- Starveling as Moonshine at least tries to deliver his set lines poetically, but he's undermined by his stage audience, who can't contain their witty interjections. Moon imagery dominates much of the play, and is now incorporated into a final comic scene.
- Bottom as Pyramus destroys the moment by praising the moon's 'sunny beams' (l.256). His 'death' is a tour de force for the actor, with alliteration, repetition and extravagant gestures.

Hippolyta is exasperated by 'the silliest stuff that ever I heard' (l.204) but Theseus responds with a serious comment about acting, indicating a mellowing in his thinking: it's all 'shadows' (l.205) and requires an imaginative effort on the viewer's part. Then, when Bottom makes his 'heroic' stage death, Hippolyta looks for a moment with genuine 'pity' (l.274).

Although actors may throw away Thisbe's death scene as more absurd comedy, audiences (onstage and in the auditorium) often stop laughing when Flute tries his best to be authentic in the moment of Thisbe's death. A serious point can be made: the watching lovers see what could have resulted from their quarrels and paternal objections if things had not been resolved.

After Theseus sends the human couples to bed, the mood darkens, signalled by Puck's trochaic 'fairy speech' as he sweeps the floor. It's an invitation to watch another kind of play, this time a blessing ritual, to be performed by Titania and Oberon dancing together.

Puck's emphasis on 'now' (l.349–68) is a reminder that night, although full of fearful things for mortals, is the natural habitat of fairies, who operate ambiguously for good and ill within the dark side, following the moon's chariot ('triple Hecate's team', l.362). Every human in this house is safely under fairy protection.

Titania takes up the rhythm, her verse more graceful and lilting, encouraging the dance, which Oberon joins as he casts a protective spell to bless the married couples and the health of their future children.

Puck's epilogue

Puck is left alone onstage to break the dramatic spell that has bound the theatre audience to the play's action. This is always a powerful emotional moment in the theatre because Puck breaks the illusion in a way that exposes the rich layering of dramatic experience – the more an audience has been involved, the harder it is to let go and wake from the 'dream'.

Puck becomes all the more 'real' to us as he urges us to be tolerant of shadows (both actors and fairies) or, if we can't do that, we can dismiss the play as just a dream. 'Give me your hands' (l.415) is a farewell gesture of friendship as well as an invitation to applaud.

Q Are Theseus' words 'very notably discharged' (l.339) patronising, or is this genuine praise – has the Mechanicals' performance made him consider things a bit more?

Q 'There is not one word apt, one player fitted' (l.65) is Philostrate's assessment of the Mechanicals' play. Do you agree?

Q How does Puck reveal his darker associations in his epilogue?

CHARACTERS & RELATIONSHIPS

Theseus and Hippolyta

Key quotes

Theseus:	Hippolyta, I wooed thee with my sword, And won thy love doing thee injuries ... (1.1.16–17)
Theseus:	I never may believe These antique fables, nor these fairy toys. (5.1.2–3)
Hippolyta:	Four days will quickly steep themselves in night; Four nights will quickly dream away the time ... (1.1.7–8)
Hippolyta:	'Tis strange, my Theseus, that these lovers speak of. (5.1.1)

The marriage of these two noble characters is the framing story in the play, but they appear in only three scenes. Theseus' idea of wooing Hippolyta is to make a grand public show of their wedding. Although his manner is courteous, we sense that the union is intended politically to secure a peace and 'bond of fellowship' (1.1.85), as well as to celebrate love.

Hippolyta is a war trophy rather than (at least initially) a beloved bride, which partly accounts for her near silence in the first scene with Theseus. She does not intervene to support or defend Hermia, but an implicit stage direction in Theseus' question 'what cheer, my love?' (1.1.122) indicates she is not happy.

Theseus is the controlling partner – he speaks, he decides, he plays the part of the rational male Athenian ruler whose word is law. He can't understand how the lovers have found concord (harmony) after fighting (although he might look to his own changed experience with his Amazon enemy/partner) and refuses to accept absurd old stories and supernatural explanations ('fairy toys', 5.1.3) for strange things that happen.

Hippolyta is less sceptical than Theseus. Like him, she knows about power and violence, and has exercised royal control over her own people, but she has a different view of natural rhythms and inexplicable experiences, allowing the moon, night and dream to shape her perceptions. She not only tolerates paradox and strangeness but is intrigued by the lovers' stories, sensing that a more-than-rational explanation can be found somewhere. Do Theseus and Hippolyta have similar views about anything except hunting dogs?

We get a different impression of Theseus and Hippolyta from Oberon and Titania's discussion of them in 2.1. Shakespeare's audience would have been familiar with the story of Theseus, Ariadne and the Minotaur, told by Ovid in *Metamorphoses*. Half bull and half man, the imprisoned Minotaur was the 'unnatural' child of the king's wife Pasiphaë and a white bull from the sea sent by the god Poseidon. Theseus killed the Minotaur and took away the Minotaur's half-sister, Ariadne, who had helped the hero for love. Returning to Athens, Theseus abandoned Ariadne on the island of Naxos, where she was rescued by the god Dionysus and became his immortal consort in Greek dramatic festivals. Ariadne is named in Oberon's list of Theseus' jilted women (2.1.78–80).

Theseus and Philostrate

Key quotes

Theseus: What masque, what music? How shall we beguile
The lazy time if not with some delight? (5.1.40–1)

Theseus: Merry and tragical? Tedious and brief?
That is hot ice and wondrous strange snow!
How shall we find the concord of this discord? (5.1.58–60)

Philostrate: For in all the play
There is not one word apt, one player fitted. (5.1.64–5)

Philostrate: It is not for you. I have heard it over,
And it is nothing, nothing in the world,
Unless you can find sport in their intents … (5.1.77–9)

Philostrate is Theseus' servant, but he exercises some power as Theseus' 'usual manager of mirth' (5.1.35) because he selects the entertainments from which Theseus can choose.

Theseus has firmly conservative views on the imagination, but we discover that he likes plays and music, particularly when they are composed to celebrate his own triumphs or help him curb his impatient desire to consummate his marriage (he resents 'the anguish of a torturing hour', 5.1.37). He has a personal interest in the items being offered because, as a hero who is related to Hercules, he's already boasted to Hippolyta about his kinsman's exploits.

The 'tedious brief scene' (5.1.56), which Philostrate tries to dismiss as 'nothing', leads Theseus to again confront the paradox about concord with discord he encountered intellectually but couldn't resolve when the young lovers were found in 4.1. Perhaps he learns a different way of thinking from the Mechanicals' play – his observation that 'love ... and tongue-tied simplicity / In least speak most' (5.1.104–5) suggests that he might.

Oberon and Titania

Key quotes

Oberon:	Why should Titania cross her Oberon? (2.1.119)
Oberon:	What thou seest when thou dost wake, Do it for thy true love take; Love and languish for his sake. (2.2.33–5)
Oberon:	Her dotage now I do begin to pity ... (4.1.44)
Titania:	I have foresworn his bed and company. (2.1.62)
Titania:	My Oberon, what visions have I seen! Methought I was enamoured of an ass. (4.1.73–4)
Titania:	Hand in hand with fairy grace Will we sing and bless this place. (5.1.377–8)

Oberon and Titania are often doubled with Theseus and Hippolyta in performance, allowing actors to explore their characters' alter egos. Both the human and the fairy couple experience discord but the dynamics of their relationships are quite different.

Oberon is described by Puck as 'passing fell and wrath' (2.1.20) because he has demanded but failed to get his hands on the Indian boy Titania is protecting. Oberon can't understand why she is refusing to share his bed and thinks it's all her fault that the natural world is so disturbed by their quarrelling. Why does he think of her wilfulness as a personal 'injury' (2.1.147) that needs to be revenged by tormenting her in a humiliating way?

Think about the events of 2.2 as a violation of the fairies' protective lullaby – 'Never harm / Nor spell nor charm / Come our lovely lady nigh' (2.2.16–18) – which they sing only moments before Oberon easily enters Titania's bower. Is this a comic moment or not? Why is the fairy charm ineffective?

Oberon and Titania are fiery and strong-willed, and have caused some humans to be unfaithful and betrayed. We could think of these powerful fairies as demonstrating how people might behave if they were allowed to run wild and act on their desires without consequences. The fairies test boundaries that human beings understand and respect as husband and wife, lord and lady. They also have power to confer gifts on mortals and, once their own relationship is mended, Oberon and Titania fill Theseus' palace with sung and danced blessings as the play ends.

Puck and Oberon

Key quotes

Puck:	I am that merry wanderer of the night. I jest to Oberon, and make him smile ... (2.1.43–4)
Puck:	Lord, what fools these mortals be! (3.2.115)
Oberon:	This is thy negligence. Still thou mistak'st, Or else committ'st thy knaveries wilfully. (3.2.345–6)

Shakespeare brings together the well-known character of Puck, also called Robin Goodfellow, from British folklore, and Oberon from

European fairy romances to create a pair of supernatural tricksters. The relationship between Puck, a servant but also a free agent, and his powerful master is intimate, volatile and entertaining.

Puck delights in avoiding punishment for causing mayhem, making sport of his accidents and mischief. He also expresses another side to his folk personality, declaring that he is 'feared in field and town' (3.2.398) and making sinister comments about shapeshifting (2.1.44–57) as well as ghosts and the unhappy dead (3.2.381–4 and 5.1.357–60). However, Oberon responds by stressing that they 'are spirits of another sort' (3.2.388). He redirects Puck's dark magic positively – to keep the angry lovers safely apart by deliberately changing the weather to obscure everything, and then to wear them out so that Puck can administer the antidote herb to heal Lysander's delusion.

Titania and Bottom

Key quotes

Titania:	What angel wakes me from my flowery bed? (3.1.107)
Titania:	Out of this wood do not desire to go: Thou shalt remain here, whether thou wilt or no. (3.1.126–7)
Titania:	Methought I was enamoured of an ass. (4.1.74)
Bottom:	This is to make an ass of me, to fright me, if they could ... (3.1.99–100)
Bottom:	Methought I was – and methought I had – but man is but a patched fool if he will offer to say what methought I had. (4.1.203–5)
Bottom:	Masters, I am to discourse wonders – but ask me not what; for if I tell you, I am not true Athenian. (4.2.22–3)

When Puck tells Oberon that 'my mistress with a monster is in love' (3.2.6) he is not just reporting a grossly comic love mismatch he's helped to bring about. Behind Bottom's transformation into a silly but sexually potent donkey-man stands another shadowy creature, the Minotaur of

Crete, which Shakespeare's audience would have associated with the Theseus and Ariadne story.

Bottom is the comic antithesis of the bull-man Minotaur; he's goofy, passive and unthreatening, an ordinary Athenian weaver who suddenly finds himself talking to the Fairy Queen. She speaks poetic verse; he speaks down-to-earth prose. In their first conversation he still has enough grasp on the real world to point out to Titania that she has no reason to be so suddenly enthralled with him.

Key point

When Bottom makes his observation about 'reason and love keep[ing] little company together' (3.1.120), he's saying something very wise in terms of what Shakespeare's entire play is working towards – a way of resolving discord by uniting apparent opposites into one imaginative concord through a dramatic plot.

Titania's urgent desire for Bottom is sensual and sexual: she decorates his head and big ears with flowers and leads him away to her bed, crooning to him, 'Oh, how I love thee! How I dote on thee!' (4.1.42). As the dominant partner, she forbids him to leave the wood but, even though besotted, she seems to realise her new lover needs to be purged of his 'mortal grossness' (3.1.134).

Does Bottom ever realise that he is changed in appearance and wonder why his appetite has been adjusted to desire oats, peas and a bottle of hay? By 4.1, as he settles comfortably into his donkey personality, being scratched and groomed by fairies, Titania becomes even more romantically poetic.

When she is released from her spell, Titania is repelled by the 'ass' she sees, and thinks it all a puzzling lapse in memory that Oberon will be able to explain to her (4.1.97–9). For Bottom, the experience of his enchantment is more profound and lasting even though he can't articulate it sensibly except as a dream.

The attendant fairies

Peaseblossom, Cobweb, Moth and **Mustardseed** were traditionally played by children, with a balletic style and flowery costumes. Nowadays they are usually played by robust adult actors, often doubling with the Mechanicals for extra comic effect – Bottom may half-recognise them and react as though he's hallucinating.

Shakespeare's fairies are robust, whimsical, dangerous if crossed, and busy in the natural world. This is how the Elizabethan audience would have understood the power of unseen forces around them. Look carefully at how the mortal and fairy worlds interact in the play, whether humans are consciously aware of it or not. The lustful, angry, jealous relationships in the fairy world mirror those in the human world.

Theseus and Egeus: patriarchy against Hermia

Key quotes

Egeus: I beg the ancient privilege of Athens;
As she is mine, I may dispose of her ... (1.1.41–2)

Theseus: To you your father should be as a god ... (1.1.47)

Hermia: So will I grow, so live, so die, my lord,
Ere I will yield my virgin patent up
Unto his lordship, whose unwishèd yoke
My soul consents not to give sovereignty. (1.1.79–82)

Theseus: For you, fair Hermia, look you arm yourself
To fit your fancies to your father's will;
Or else the law of Athens yields you up
(Which by no means we may extenuate)
To death, or to a vow of single life. (1.1.117–21)

In Shakespeare's time, especially among well-connected merchant or aristocratic families, it was expected that fathers would exercise control over who their children selected as partners in order to make advantageous marriages. The first scene is disturbing because Egeus forcefully asserts his absolute right to make his daughter marry a partner of *his* choice, not *hers*. His will is paramount and he considers that Lysander has cheated him personally and stolen his property.

Look carefully at the way Theseus argues for the strict Athenian law to uphold patriarchal rights but still presses Hermia to take the blame as if she's the one at fault for selfishly following her 'fancies' (her own desires). While he praises 'single blessedness' (1.1.78) – after all, a fiercely virgin Queen Elizabeth I was on the throne in England at the time – his choice of words such as 'barren', 'faint hymns', 'cold fruitless moon' and 'withering' (1.1.172–7) reveal what a low value he puts on female virginity as a life choice, when Hermia could instead enjoy being a 'rose distilled' (1.1.76) in a socially approved marriage.

Given this weight of opposition, Hermia's public defiance is very brave. She speaks up to defend her 'virgin patent' (her rights to her own body, 1.1.80) as a love gift from her soul, not as her father's commodity to trade with Demetrius.

The young Athenian lovers

Hermia and Lysander

Key quotes

Hermia:	Since night you loved me; yet since night you left me. (3.2.275)
Lysander:	Not Hermia, but Helena I love. Who will not change a raven for a dove? (2.2.119–20)

Because Lysander expresses such genuinely loving concern for Hermia, and offers a practical escape from her father's dominance, she puts all her faith in him. Their key duologue (1.1.128–49) about what can obstruct 'the course of true love' (l.134) underlines the fragility and vulnerability of love's feelings, 'short as any dream' (l.144) and devoured by 'the jaws of darkness' (l.148). That catastrophe nearly happens when Lysander is charmed by the love juice to abandon Hermia for Helena and claims his newly understood 'reason' is giving him what he wants (2.2.121–6).

Lysander's reversal is so shocking to Hermia that she ends the big quarrel scene speechless, sometimes turning to the audience for 'I am amazed, and know not what to say' (3.2.344). This is a laugh line even while we feel pity for her.

Helena and Demetrius

Key quotes

Helena:	I am your spaniel; and, Demetrius, The more you beat me I will fawn on you. (2.1.203–4)
Demetrius:	I love thee not, therefore pursue me not. (2.1.188)

In Helena's pursuit of Demetrius, Shakespeare reverses a traditional Petrarchan love trope (image or idea): ardent man pursues, cruel mistress resists and denies (see page 55 for more on the Italian poet Petrarch). Helena feels mocked and shamed by both men in 3.2: this is her lowest point, and she has no way of understanding the situation except that she admits she pursued Demetrius into the woods to spoil Lysander and Hermia's plan. We cringe at her absurd desire to be her lover's mistreated 'spaniel', but it shows how desperate she is to be noticed by him.

Both men go through a deranged Petrarchan stage (with overblown language and expressions of extreme, intense emotion) before coming back to loving their partners realistically. Demetrius describes his returning love for Helena as though it's a recovery of appetite after sickness, 'as in health come to my natural taste' (4.1.171).

Hermia and Helena

Key quotes

Hermia:	I am amazèd at your passionate words. I scorn you not; it seems that you scorn me. (3.2.220–1)
Helena:	Fie, fie, you counterfeit, you puppet, you! (3.2.288)

Shakespeare frames Hermia and Helena's broken friendship in terms of comedy, leading us to enjoy the inventiveness of their pointed insults, spiteful comparisons, accusations and threats of physical violence in 3.2. When we look beneath the comedy we recognise two perplexed young women, neither of whom understands what has happened to change their men.

Initially, Helena is so distressed to have been rejected that she wants to erase her own features completely and *become* Hermia, if that's what will attract Demetrius. She thinks of herself as a frightening monster, 'ugly as a bear' (2.2.100), thereby excusing Demetrius for leaving her alone at night in the wood. Then, when both Demetrius and Lysander declare their love for her, she feels mocked and abused. Of the four, she is the most emotionally damaged and vulnerable.

Lysander and Demetrius

Key quotes

Lysander:	Demetrius, I'll avouch it to his head, Made love to Nedar's daughter, Helena, And won her soul; and she, sweet lady, dotes, Devoutly dotes, dotes in idolatry, Upon this spotted and inconstant man. (1.1.106–10)
Demetrius:	Relent, sweet Hermia; and, Lysander, yield Thy crazèd title to my certain right. (1.1.91–2)

These two young men are equally eligible but not interchangeable – even when bewitched – because they are loved by different women who don't change their affections. Look carefully at the lovers' harmonious reunion in 4.1 (from line 138). All the lovers are puzzled by what has happened. Throughout the night the women have remained faithful to their original lovers, but the men have flipped.

THEMES, IDEAS & VALUES

Although this section contains notes under a number of broad theme headings as though each theme is a separate set of ideas, none of them exist in isolation. The interplay between themes and the clash of ideas, values and questions they generate is what makes *A Midsummer Night's Dream* so intriguing and dramatically exciting to study.

Love

Key quote

Lysander:	The course of true love never did run smooth ... (1.1.134)

A Midsummer Night's Dream asks serious questions about love but explores them in a safe space of comedy with an assured happy ending.

Ways of experiencing love

Shakespeare's audience knew many ways of describing different types of love from myths, romances and philosophy, even if they didn't know all the proper classical terms. As we read this play it's helpful to remember the subtle variations on what love means, all of which we can find in our own experience.

Eros is irrational, dangerous, madness-inducing and uncontrolled; it encompasses erotic love, romance and sexual passion. The characters imagine a god of love called Cupid, the son of Venus, in Roman mythology; or Eros, son of Aphrodite, in Greek mythology (from which we get the word 'erotic'). Shakespeare's idea of Cupid as a 'knavish lad' (3.2.440) whose random wounding with golden arrows of desire or leaden arrows of despair, leading people to fall madly in love, was something ancient Greeks had been wary about, too. *Eros* is about expressing and satisfying desire and lust as well as honourable and chaste romantic feelings for someone. The fairy magic amplifies already strong emotional urges that are natural to young people like Hermia, Lysander, Helena and Demetrius.

The 'Pyramus and Thisbe' story (found in Ovid's *Metamorphoses*) shows what could happen to love that doesn't find fulfilment or social approval. Helena describes Cupid as traditionally 'painted blind' (1.1.235) and expands on what that means for hapless humans who are shot with his arrows of desire for good or ill. Hermia swears her love to Lysander by invoking the golden arrows of the same blind god: 'I swear to thee by Cupid's strongest bow' (1.1.169). She desires her lover but wants to act modestly until their marriage. Puck makes a false assumption that Lysander isn't sexually amorous enough, calling him 'this lack-love, this kill-courtesy' (2.2.83) when he sees the lovers sleeping separately in the wood. This is comic dramatic irony because we know Hermia had to argue forcefully to convince Lysander not to sleep too close to her, despite his gentlemanly protestations.

Theseus reveals his own frustrated desire in 1.1, and also presents Hermia with a negative idea of chastity as a consequence if she refuses to marry Demetrius. What do Theseus' words tell us about his attitude to chaste resistance to *eros*, especially in women? Theseus was well known in Elizabethan times as a serial seducer and deserter – information that is implicit in Oberon and Titania's conversation in 2.1 (especially lines 77–80).

Philia is non-erotic but strong love for close friends and colleagues. It involves loyalty, sharing emotions, truthfulness and a willingness to sacrifice oneself for another. This is the love invoked by genuine mateship, and the moving 'no greater love' theme of remembrance. This was a closeness highly prized by heroes, and Shakespeare treats this form of love both seriously *and* comically.

- Helena appeals to Hermia's memories of friendship and loyalty in a long, detailed speech, appealing to *philia* even in comic excess (3.2.195–219).
- The Mechanicals express their bond with each other and pride in their project.

Storge (pronounced *store-jay*) is familial love: the way a parent loves their children. It is instinctive and protective, but can cause intergenerational problems.

- Egeus may be regarded nowadays as having a distorted idea of parental love, accusing Hermia of disobedience.
- Oberon and Titania quarrel over the Indian boy she stole from his father – are their feelings parental?
- Titania cuddles Bottom and lulls him to sleep like her big baby.
- Pyramus and Thisbe face parental opposition, forcing them to meet secretly.

Ludus is playful love (the Latin word *ludus* means game) – it encompasses teasing, flirting, playing silly (ludicrous) jokes on friends, dancing frivolously with strangers. It can be a playful substitute for sex or making sexual adventures a game.

Puck sees humans as fair game for teasing because they are so easily fooled. Even when he accepts he's made a mistake with the love potion, causing 'some true love turned, and not a false turned true' (3.2.91), he's cynically aware that humans are likely to treat love like a game and be unfaithful without his meddling: 'Then fate o'errules, that, one man holding troth, / A million fail, confounding oath on oath' (3.2.92–3).

Philautia is self-love. In its positive form it means loving yourself, having self-respect, feeling confident, being secure in yourself and caring for yourself, which opens you to love that is offered and projects a love that is attractive to others. In negative forms it is narcissism, being self-obsessed. It can also be experienced negatively when the feeling is reversed as a loss of self-worth, insecurity or feelings of lovelessness or unworthiness.

Unrequited love may encourage masochism, leading to painful doting (being obsessed by the one you love, whether they return your affection or not). Helena feels utterly devalued as a result of being jilted by Demetrius. She feels ugly, worthless and unlovable, taking the blame for his change of sentiment (after he had previously 'won her soul', 1.1.108).

Mania results from obsessive love thoughts, stalking and doting; it can manifest in murderous jealousy of a rival, especially if one is rejected or jilted.

- Helena betrays Hermia and Lysander to Demetrius, knowing he'll chase after them to get Hermia back – giving Helena an excuse to chase after him.
- Oberon's revenge on Titania is obsessive and angry because she won't give up the boy he wants as his 'henchman' (follower, 2.1.121).
- Titania's doting on Bottom is comic because it is excessively attentive to an absurd love object, which she can't see because of the love charm.

Love and marriage

Puck declares that 'Jack shall have Jill' (3.2.461), but how might that be problematic now? Should love and marriage be linked together? In Shakespeare's time the state religion (the Church of England) made money out of sanctioning church unions between heterosexual couples who had already made a commitment by handfasting – exchanging vows and joining hands before friends as witnesses. Many brides were already pregnant when they went to the altar for their formal church wedding. Shakespeare isn't mocking romantic love that leads to marriage but *testing* it.

Marriage was and is a social construct reinforced by law, but laws can change as people change and grow in understanding. Recent productions of *A Midsummer Night's Dream* have opened up some alternatives to the exclusively heterosexual couplings in Shakespeare's text.

You could argue that Shakespeare uses the pairing of Theseus and Hippolyta, and, more dynamically, of Oberon and Titania, to model how **pragmatic love**, a long-term commitment where partners both make the effort to stay together, learning to accommodate and tolerate each other's differences, is a feature of mature, realistic relationships. It involves continuing and genuine care for a partner after the excitement stage of 'falling in love' has waned or when fidelity is tested. There may never be a perfect romantic match.

Reason and imagination

Key quotes

Lysander:	The will of man is by his reason swayed ... (2.2.121)
Theseus:	Lovers and madmen have such seething brains, Such shaping fantasies, that apprehend More than cool reason ever comprehends. ... And as imagination bodies forth The forms of things unknown, the poet's pen Turns them to shapes, and gives to airy nothing A local habitation and a name. (5.1.4–6, 14–17)
Bottom:	... reason and love keep little company together nowadays ... (3.1.120–1)

Athenian rationality

If Athens is held up as a symbol of classical reason and civilisation, it validates patriarchal norms relating to law and order: men are in charge and make judgements; women are obedient. *A Midsummer Night's Dream* challenges these assumptions in several ways, especially when free choice collides with patriarchal law. Self-interested or faulty judgement might be interrogated; for example, Lysander's assertion that he 'had no judgement' when he loved Hermia is rightly challenged by Helena (3.2.134–5).

Notice how Theseus' concept of Athenian law (1.1.117–21) is essentially identical to patriarchal will, against which Hermia's 'fancies' are unfairly rendered inadmissible. However, Shakespeare gives Hermia, Helena and Titania strong, challenging characters who behave contrary to expected norms for women as partners to men.

The wild wood at night is set against Athens as a powerful alternative location to encounter laws and choices; it is a place where imagination and fairy magic can undermine 'cool reason' with dreams and illusions. Demetrius correctly puns on being 'wood' (mad) 'within this wood' (2.1.192) as he chases distractedly after Hermia. In contrast, Lysander speaks confidently about being led by his 'reason' (2.2.121–6) but we know he's acting irrationally under the influence of the love spell. He gets the connection between 'reason' and 'will' the wrong way round because he's driven by desire and tricked by magic. Yet as an Athenian he feels compelled to attribute his actions to reason, hence his distorted argument.

Reason and imagination for Elizabethans

Reason deals in facts, reality, hierarchy and social stratification (classes). **Imagination** encourages fancy, fantasy, creativity and emotions like love, but can also lead to lies, mistaking, delusions, confusion and disorder. Do you agree this is so clearcut?

In Shakespeare's time, Reason was given precedence over Imagination, which was closely connected to Dreaming (during which imagination or 'fancy' was not restricted by rationality). Elizabethan psychology had complex ways of understanding the near-synonymous terms Fantasy, Fancy and Imagination, often supposing that Imagination or 'feigning' led to deranged ideas about reality and was not to be trusted by the superior faculty of reason coupled with judgement.

It was a big debate and Shakespeare was engrossed in it, reading the latest translations from French theorists like Pierre de La Primaudaye (translated and for sale in London in 1594). He borrowed ideas and even specialised vocabulary like 'feigning' and 'forgeries' from contemporary psychological works to put into *A Midsummer Night's Dream*.

Can reason and love coexist?

Elizabethan critics of imaginative writing targeted the experience of love as being particularly susceptible to corrupting fantasy. *A Midsummer Night's Dream* is Shakespeare's way of exploring that idea and defending the other side of the argument – he suggests that 'feigning' as Imagination under the control of the creative writer unites Reason and Imagination as Poetic Truth and can restore reason and love in a healthy relationship.

The play sets out love madness to demonstrate that the poet's creative control over fantasy is helpful and entertaining, and to encourage us to think more about how we plunge into life with one another. It can be argued that this is the point of creative art – to reveal higher truths.

Theseus thinks he's the spokesman for accepted rationality: he links the lunatic, the lover and the poet, although each experiences imagination differently. Look carefully at each step in his key speech (5.1.2–22). Does the play support his argument at all?

Shakespeare is also reflecting on how his own art comes into being, and how his imagination gives shape to 'the forms of things unknown' (5.1.15). He constructs characters who have conversations about perplexing feelings and thoughts, to explore their imaginations together. We, as readers and audience, may learn from what we hear and see in a play that makes space for dreams as authentic representations of non-rational processes.

You could argue that Shakespeare's spokesman is Bottom, a genuinely simple but wise ass: he knows Titania 'should have little reason' to suddenly fall in love with him. Look carefully at his key speech (3.1.119–22). Shakespeare the playwright is one of the 'honest neighbours' trying to make reason and love compatible.

Fears change rational perceptions to irrational imaginings

Key quotes

Puck: Their sense thus weak, lost with their fears thus strong,
Made senseless things begin to do them wrong ... (3.2.27–8)

Theseus: Or in the night, imagining some fear,
How easy is a bush supposed a bear? (5.1.21–2)

How do the play's characters try to apply reason to puzzle out inexplicable things that are emotionally upsetting? They don't have the full picture, but we do – Shakespeare lets us retain a comic perspective through dramatic irony, while Puck lets us revel with him in the irrational mayhem he's spread around. Helena assumes the other lovers are playing a horrible trick on her (3.2.145–6), while Bottom thinks his mates are trying to frighten him (3.1.94–5). They are in situations where reasoning is ineffective, allowing fear to dominate thoughts and feelings.

Dreams

Key quotes

Oberon:	When they next wake, all this derision Shall seem a dream and fruitless vision … (3.2.370–1)
Oberon:	And think no more of this night's accidents But as the fierce vexation of a dream. (4.1.65–6)
Puck:	And this weak and idle theme, No more yielding but a dream … (5.1.405–6)

In Shakespeare's time, dreams were taken seriously by many and shared, remembered and interpreted: what dreams could tell everybody was backed up by a long tradition of dream books, medical treatises and scholarship. Not everyone was in agreement. Some people regarded dreams as seriously predictive, while for others they were merely a result of bad digestion after dinner – this was the opinion of Thomas Nashe, a fellow playwright, who wrote a sceptical pamphlet in 1594 titled *The Terrors of the Night*. Nashe was dismissive of 'Robin Goodfellows, elves, fairies, hobgoblins' (Nashe 1594, p.5) and defined most dreams as 'nothing else but a bubbling scum or froth of the fancy which the day hath left undigested, or an after-feast made of the fragments of idle imagination' (p.10). Shakespeare took some of his ideas from Nashe, especially for Theseus in 5.1.

Experiencing the dream

Notice how senses get confused in dreams – we can't assess what we're seeing and hearing. Points of view shift in dreams, too; sometimes we are participants, sometimes we are observers, and often we are both, stepping in and out of the dream story as time shifts occur.

The lovers emerging from the wood hardly know what happened to them. Were they only dreaming, or did they actually experience turbulent emotional shifts? It needs talking about, as Demetrius suggests while they walk back to the real world of Athens: 'And by the way let us recount our dreams' (4.1.196). Hippolyta picks up this idea when she comments to Theseus (5.1.23–7) that the lovers have experienced something beyond conscious explanations.

The only actual dream described in the play is Hermia's (2.2.151–6) and it may be the predictive kind. She wakes up in terror, feeling she is being attacked by a serpent that eats her heart while Lysander smiles, not helping her. What do you think she might be fearing subconsciously? Why is the snake such a strong image for the imagination?

The image of the snake stays with her when she confronts Demetrius about killing Lysander (3.2.70–3), accusing him of being a cowardly deceitful adder. So is Demetrius the serpent in her dream? Then Lysander calls *her* a serpent that he will shake off (3.2.261), distressing her further.

Look for many more references to dreams in the play and discover how Shakespeare is exploring different ideas relating to states of mind or inexplicable events, such as:

- Hippolyta in a dreamy mood – 'Four nights will quickly dream away the time' (1.1.8)
- Lysander thinking of love's vulnerability – 'short as any dream' (1.1.144)
- Bottom after his brief affair with Titania – 'I have had a most rare vision' (4.1.200).

Shakespeare tantalises us playfully with ideas about what we've experienced in the play. Oberon and Puck comment on how we (unlike the lovers and Bottom) can dismiss the action as nothing more than a dream if we choose. A 'fruitless vision' (3.2.371)? The 'fierce vexation of a dream' (4.1.66)? A 'weak and idle theme' (5.1.405) that won't bear much scrutiny? The supernatural characters give us an option to disbelieve what *A Midsummer Night's Dream* is about, especially its serious undercurrent. Shakespeare is asking us to value dreams.

Change and transformation

Key quotes

Hermia:	Before the time I did Lysander see, Seemed Athens as a paradise to me. O then, what graces in my love do dwell, That he hath turned a heaven unto a hell? (1.1.204–7)
Helena:	Things base and vile, holding no quantity, Love can transpose to form and dignity. (1.1.232–3)
Quince:	Bless thee, Bottom, bless thee! Thou art translated! (3.1.98)

Being alive means we are all subject to change in various ways: physically (Puck reminds us about death, the ultimate change for humans), emotionally and intellectually. *A Midsummer Night's Dream* investigates how people change their opinions, preferences, beliefs and ideas of themselves.

- What if some people can't change, like Egeus, who just has to be overruled?
- How does Helena's opinion of herself undergo change? Would changing herself into a 'look and sound alike' copy of Hermia really help her to grow?
- As a result of loving Lysander, Hermia's comfortable ideas about Athens and home change radically, so that paradoxically love has turned heaven into hell for her.
- The feelings and affections of Lysander and Demetrius change dramatically in the wood. Do they find new stability by experiencing these changes?
- The Mechanicals grapple with the idea of theatre as an environment where an actor can consciously assume a character and temporarily transform into somebody else.

The moon as a symbol of change for humans

How aware are you of the changing moon? The moon is a visible object in the night sky as well as a powerful symbol of change in the natural world.

A Midsummer Night's Dream's action is framed by the old moon turning into the new moon again, and the play is metaphorically saturated in moonlight imagery and references to myths about moon goddesses.

Starveling enacts 'the man in the moon' as an absurdly costumed emblem of an old story. He tries to give dignity to his part but is constantly interrupted by witty heckling from the courtly audience. Even Hippolyta's sharp joke about being 'aweary of this moon' (5.1.238) underlines its inept representation.

Shape changing

Puck is accomplished at shapeshifting, which he does for sheer merriment. Find his many kinds of transformations to entertain Oberon (2.1.44–57) and torment the panicked Mechanicals (3.1.90–3).

Two other significant ideas about transformation are explored through Bottom and Helena. Bottom's transformation, a combination of rude hilarity tinged with romantic pathos (because his affair with Titania can only be a momentary one), is the change everyone remembers from *A Midsummer Night's Dream*. Shakespeare borrowed from a well-known classical story, *The Golden Ass* (by the ancient Roman writer Apuleius, translated into English in 1566 by Richard Adlington), in which the protagonist, Lucius, is transformed into an ass. He also knew contemporary accounts of Robin Goodfellow and transformation spells in pamphlets and Scot's *The Discoverie of Witchcraft* (published in 1584). Scot wrote sceptically about reports of men being turned into asses and other absurd terrors experienced by 'sicke folke, children, women, and cowards, which through weaknesse of mind and bodie, are shaken with vaine dreames and continuall feare', adding something Shakespeare might have picked up: 'we are afraid of our owne shadowes' (Scot 1886, Book VII, Chapter XV).

Embraced by the Fairy Queen and restored to his human shape by simple magic, Bottom is the only mortal in the play to interact with the fairy world. Oberon instructs Puck to release Bottom so that he will not be permanently changed by his experience except to recall it as the 'fierce vexation of a dream' (4.1.66).

Helena strongly desires to be changed by magic into the woman Demetrius finds attractive. Her exhausted misery makes her perceive herself as already changed into a deformed monster. Because she imagines that she is 'as ugly as a bear' (so it's her fault) she excuses the man who has rejected her (2.2.100–3), but to whom she was previously 'betrothed' (4.1.169). We can laugh at Helena's wallowing in self-pity while we are also aware that her obsession reveals how deeply her identity has been challenged.

Eyes and seeing

Key quotes

Hermia:	I would my father looked but with my eyes. (1.1.56)
Helena:	Your virtue is my privilege: for that It is not night when I do see your face, Therefore I think I am not in the night … (2.1.220–2)
Demetrius:	To what, my love, shall I compare thine eyne? (3.2.138)
Oberon:	Be as thou wast wont to be; See as thou wast wont to see. (4.1.68–9)

The facts that people perceive things differently and that they cannot know what others see shape ideas about love in *A Midsummer Night's Dream*. Elizabethan psychology basically taught that reasonable perceptions are formed by what the eye takes in and transmits via the other senses to the mind for processing. Faulty vision leads to mental error, leading to imaginary 'fancies', emotional confusion and untruths.

This is likely to happen when love, personified as 'blind Cupid', encourages lovers to bypass the checking process from eye to mind, or when the 'love-in-idleness' flower spell takes over (2.1.168). Oberon's healing herb, restoring chaste sight, is appropriately 'Dian's bud' (Diana was a virgin goddess in Roman mythology, 4.1.70) which has 'blessèd power' (4.1.71) to take 'all error' (3.2.368) and 'hateful imperfection' (4.1.60) from bewitched eyes.

When the lovers are most confused by spells, they revert to familiar Elizabethan ideas about beloved eyes, often found in Petrarchan love poetry. The Italian poet Petrarch (1304–1374) wrote sonnets addressed to an idealised but unobtainable woman called Laura, in which erotic charge is enhanced by frustration. Shakespeare uses Petrarchan images because they are comically excessive.

- Helena doesn't see night as threatening or lonely because Demetrius brings 'all the world' to her (2.1.224): 'It is not night when I do see your face' (2.1.221).
- Lysander instantly targets Helena's eyes as 'Love's stories written in love's richest book' (2.2.128). She's just been moping about her own tear-washed eyes compared to 'Hermia's sphery eyne' (2.1.105).
- Demetrius comes to his senses and declares Helena to be 'the object and the pleasure of mine eye' (4.1.167).
- 'So is mine eye enthrallèd to thy shape' says Titania to Bottom (3.1.116). To be enthralled means literally to be a slave (thrall), often by magic. Compare this with her unenchanted sight: 'O, how mine eyes do loathe his visage now!' (4.1.76).

Playing and performance

Key quotes

Puck:	What, a play toward? I'll be an auditor, An actor too perhaps, if I see cause. (3.1.62–3)
Theseus:	What masque, what music? How shall we beguile The lazy time if not with some delight? (5.1.40–1)
Quince:	If we offend, it is with our good will. (5.1.108)

Shakespeare is fascinated by connotations of the word 'play' and works related ideas into *A Midsummer Night's Dream*, a comedy about playing, with Puck as a feral 'stage manager' and Oberon directing much of the action. Yet Shakespeare has a creative grasp of what a play is on the page and in performance, and what it can conjure up for an audience.

He lets us know that plays are not just imaginative fictions to 'beguile the lazy time', and *A Midsummer Night's Dream* helps us to consider the relationship between the world of the play and real-world activities and issues.

The play within the play

Shakespeare embeds 'Pyramus and Thisbe' into the main drama for several reasons. These include:

- to show the young Athenian lovers what could happen if they don't resolve issues and agree to live sociably
- to show readers and audiences how unsophisticated conventions inhibit the kind of illusion, subtle characterisation through dialogue and complex storytelling that Shakespeare aims for.

The Mechanicals mimic old-style players like those Shakespeare may have seen performing at Stratford or nearby Coventry when he was growing up. Their earnest attention to illusion-destroying details, discussion of correct-coloured beards (1.2.71–6) and a rude joke about 'French crowns' (a reference to a loss of hair from venereal disease, 1.2.77) would have been crowd-pleasers for an audience that was becoming attuned to Shakespeare's more sophisticated drama.

Shadows: actors and fairies

Key quotes

Puck:	Believe me, King of Shadows, I mistook. (3.2.347)
Theseus:	The best in this kind are but shadows; and the worst are no worse, if imagination amend them. (5.1.205–6)
Puck:	If we shadows have offended … (5.1.401)

For Elizabethans, 'shadows' meant unreal representations of different kinds. Shakespeare uses the word in *A Midsummer Night's Dream* to underline important ideas about the supernatural, imagination and theatre as a mimetic art, an imitation of reality.

- Puck calls Oberon 'King of Shadows' to reinforce the Fairy King's unlimited and fearsome power to move invisibly in and out of the natural world.
- Theseus is referring to living actors when he uses the word, implying that *all* actors playing parts are unreal. If they perform inadequately, the audience must exercise imagination to 'amend' or supply the mimetic deficit in the show. Theseus refuses an offered 'epilogue', turning it into a joke about 'players' (both the actors *and* the characters they played) needing 'no excuse' (apology) because they are 'all dead' (5.1.335–6). Has he taken notice at all of the performers as 'shadows'?
- Puck provides an epilogue to the play because he acts as a go-between from the world of 'play' to us, the living audience. He unites the different connotations of 'we shadows' as both fairies and human characters played by actors. He also offers his own 'excuse' for the play by suggesting that the audience can dismiss it as only a dream if anything has 'offended' them. He seems to be reducing the actors to harmless, unreal 'shadows'. In fact, though, in Puck's final speech he affirms both his own reality and the magical connection that unites everyone in the theatre in a single imaginative project.

Images of nature

Key quotes

Helena: For, ere Demetrius looked on Hermia's eyne,
He hailed down oaths that he was only mine,
And when this hail some heat from Hermia felt,
So he dissolved, and showers of oaths did melt. (1.1.242–5)

Puck: When they him spy –
As wild geese that the creeping fowler eye,
Or russet-pated choughs, many in sort,
Rising and cawing at the gun's report,
Sever themselves and madly sweep the sky –
So at his sight away his fellows fly ... (3.2.20–4)

Oberon: And that same dew, which sometime on the buds
Was wont to swell like round and orient pearls,
Stood now within the pretty flowerets' eyes
Like tears that did their own disgrace bewail. (4.1.50–3)

Shakespeare draws on the natural world to create memorable imagery throughout the play.

- Helena uses a **metaphor** when she puns on the word 'hail' as meaning both to greet or acclaim someone and icy water that melts quickly (1.1.242–5).
- **Similes** compare one thing with another, as Puck does in his image of the frightened Mechanicals scattering 'as wild geese' (3.2.20).
- Oberon's description of tear-like dew droplets in pretty flowers (4.1.50–3) suggests how ashamed they feel to be decorating Bottom's ass's head. This is an example of a **pathetic fallacy** (attributing human feelings to non-human objects or living things).

Seasons, times and weather conditions are used poetically to underline how the characters are feeling and responding. For example, when Lysander asks Hermia, 'Why is your cheek so pale? / How chance the roses there do fade so fast?' (1.1.128–9), she picks up the image of wilted flowers in need of rain to describe herself.

Pastoral imagery

Pastoral literature depicts an idealised and largely peaceful view of rural life. Shakespeare's pastoral imagery in *A Midsummer Night's Dream* shows another side to Oberon's character and links the fairy world to popular Elizabethan lyrical poetry.

- Oberon's lovely image beginning 'I with the morning's love have oft made sport' (3.2.389–93), which comes straight after Puck's nightmarish description of ghosts trooping home to churchyards, reassures us that the King of Shadows has the power to cross *and* enforce barriers between worlds and make all well for mortals as the night ends.
- In their first quarrel, Titania disapproves of how Oberon 'in the shape of Corin' (a shepherd's name) has sometimes absconded from fairyland, changed shape and 'sat all day / Playing on pipes of corn, and versing love / To amorous Phillida' (a shepherdess, 2.1.66–8).
- Helena also makes her self-pitying point about Hermia's attractive singing voice in a romantically pastoral image: 'More tuneable than lark to shepherd's ear, / When wheat is green, when hawthorn buds appear' (1.1.184–5).

DIFFERENT INTERPRETATIONS

Different interpretations arise from different responses to a text. Over time, a text will evoke a wide range of responses from its readers, who may come from various social or cultural groups and live in very different places and historical periods. Responses by critics and reviewers can be published in newspapers, journals and books, both online and in print. They can also be expressed in discussions among readers in the media, classrooms, book groups and so on.

While there is no single correct reading or interpretation of a text, it is important to understand that an interpretation is more than a personal opinion – it is the justification of a point of view on the text. To present an interpretation of a text based on your point of view, you must use a logical argument and support it with relevant evidence from the text.

The critics' viewpoints

Good criticism stimulates us to ask questions and be prepared to read 'against the grain'. For example, it might invite us to critique the 'Jack shall have Jill' comic formula for a conventionally gendered happy ending, or suggest how class distinctions, patriarchal structures, cultural and historical contexts, and feminist and postcolonial ideas inform meaning in the text as you read it or see it interpreted in productions.

Nineteenth-century views of *A Midsummer Night's Dream* were dominated by Romantic ideas, reading it as funny, lyrical and innocent, and regarding it as a good way to introduce children to Shakespeare. Mendelssohn's incidental music (written mostly in the 1840s) dominated stage productions and encouraged directors to include singing and dancing by dozens of balletic fairies.

Twentieth-century and recent criticism has been divided between a continuing desire to locate a festive comic spirit in the play and a sharper critique of troubling undercurrents.

Two interpretations

The works of two twentieth-century critics, Jan Kott and CL Barber, offer very different ideas about Shakespeare's plays. Kott reads a dark vision of life while Barber finds a positive, socially affirming purpose in comedy. Both are important because they continue to influence literary critics, stage directors and filmmakers.

Reading 1

Source text: J Kott, *Shakespeare, Our Contemporary* (1964).

Jan Kott is influential because his views can be read as a necessary corrective to the decorated and romanticised fairytale world imagined by some critics and theatre productions that were a carryover from elaborate Victorian spectaculars.

The Polish teacher, writer and director lived through politically turbulent times during and after World War II, experiencing repressive Nazi and Stalinist regimes firsthand. This coloured his critical views, especially his ideas about how history works and what Shakespeare was creating. Introducing Kott's book, the director Peter Brook discussed how Kott's insights into Shakespearean drama were powerfully shaped by his life experience:

> Like Shakespeare, like Shakespeare's contemporaries, the world of the flesh and the world of the spirit are indivisible: they coexist painfully in the same frame: the poet has a foot in the mud, an eye on the stars, and a dagger in his hand ... poetry is a rough magic that fuses opposites ... It is Poland that in our time has come closest to the tumult, the danger, the intensity, the imaginativeness and the daily involvement with the social process that made life so horrible, subtle and ecstatic to an Elizabethan. So it is quite naturally up to a Pole to point us the way. (Preface, x–xi)

Kott's confronting chapter on *A Midsummer Night's Dream* is called 'Titania and the ass's head'. After naming Puck as a devil who 'liberates instincts and puts the mechanism of this world in motion. He puts it in motion and mocks it at the same time' (p.174), Kott points out that Shakespeare redirects a conventional view of comedy that links love, beauty and sensual pleasure, by substituting the 'Eros of ugliness, born through desire and culminating in folly' (p.180).

Kott references satirical drawings of donkey-humans by the Spanish artist Francisco Goya to underline the animal eroticism that drives erotic love: Titania desires the shy but sexually potent ass Bottom, while Helena yearns to be her cruel lover's physically abused spaniel:

> In the violent contrast between the erotic madness liberated by the night and the censorship of day which orders everything to be forgotten, Shakespeare seems most ahead of his time. (p.188)

The chapter concludes by pointing out that:

> The forest in Shakespeare always represents Nature ... Our instincts are also Nature. And they are as mad as the world ... The world is mad, and love is mad. In this universal madness of Nature and History, brief are the moments of happiness ... (pp.189–90)

For further reading, follow up Kott's dark reading of Shakespeare with Peter Brook's influential book *The Empty Space* (1968) on creating relevant 'Immediate Theatre'. Then find out about Brook's famous 'White Box' production of *A Midsummer Night's Dream* at Stratford in 1970.

Reading 2

Source text: CL Barber, 'May games and metamorphoses on a midsummer night', Chapter 6 in *Shakespeare's Festive Comedy. A Study of Dramatic Form and Its Relation to Social Custom* (1959).

Barber's work laid the foundation for more recent cultural and historical investigations of carnival by Michael D Bristol and Stephen Greenblatt. Barber argues that Shakespeare's comedy is basically 'festive' rather than romantic or satirical: the playwright draws on a native Saturnalian tradition of seasonal festivities, playing and merrymaking (such as May Day, Twelfth Night and Midsummer), mingling comic and serious ideas for socially productive ends. Shakespeare works out how to incorporate old festival-time rituals, games and shows into new dramatic forms for the theatre. His comedy is built imaginatively on lived experience, redefining magic as imagination, and ritual as social action.

Why is Saturnalia (from a Roman festival time in December) important and why does Shakespeare work to re-create the mood in this play, with Oberon as the Lord of Misrule and Titania as his Summer Lady? Barber's key idea is that Saturnalia releases people from the tensions and inhibitions of everyday life and, in the process, provides a twofold 'clarification' of what life means. First, it gives everyone a new awareness of nature – the natural world and what is natural in humans – while at the same time allowing people to mock the forces (laws, rules, religion, their masters) that inhibit or are opposed to pleasure and release in society. Secondly, through experiencing an intense holiday mood, people become aware of the limitations to irresponsibility and return to their everyday social reality with new understanding. So *A Midsummer Night's Dream* ends with the social order reaffirmed, as nature demands, through marriage after a period of misrule and transformation.

QUESTIONS & ANSWERS

This section focuses on your own analytical writing on the text, and gives you strategies for producing high-quality responses in your coursework and exam essays.

Essay writing – an overview

An essay on a literary work is a formal and serious piece of writing that presents your point of view on the text, usually in response to a given topic. Your 'point of view' in an essay is your interpretation of the meaning of the text's language, structure, characters, situations and events, supported by detailed analysis of textual evidence.

Analyse – don't summarise

In your essays it is important to avoid simply summarising what happens in a text.

- A **summary** is a description or paraphrase (retelling in different words) of the characters and events. For example: 'Macbeth has a horrifying vision of a dagger dripping with blood before he goes to murder King Duncan.'
- An **analysis** is an explanation of the real meaning or significance that lies 'beneath' the text's words (and images, for a film). For example: 'Macbeth's vision of a bloody dagger shows how deeply uneasy he is about the violent act he is contemplating, and conveys his sense that supernatural forces are impelling him to act.'

A limited amount of summary is sometimes necessary to let your reader know which part of the text you wish to discuss. However, always keep this to a minimum and follow it immediately with your analysis of what this part of the text is really telling us.

Plan your essay

Carefully plan your essay so that you have a clear idea of what you are going to say. The plan ensures that your ideas flow logically, that your argument remains consistent and that you stay on topic. An essay plan should be a list of **brief dot points** covering no more than half a page.

- Include your central argument or main contention – a concise statement of your overall response to the topic.
- Write three or four dot points for each paragraph, indicating the main idea and evidence/examples from the text. In your essay you will need to *expand* on these points and *analyse* the evidence.

Structure your essay

An essay is a complete, self-contained piece of writing. It has a clear beginning (the introduction), middle (several body paragraphs) and end (the last paragraph or conclusion). It must also have a central argument that runs throughout, linking each paragraph to form a coherent whole. See examples of introductions and conclusions in the 'Analysing a sample topic' and 'Sample answer' sections.

The introduction establishes your overall response to the topic. It includes your main contention and outlines the main evidence you will refer to in the course of the essay. Write your introduction *after* you have done a plan and *before* you write the rest of the essay.

The body paragraphs argue your case – they present evidence from the text and explain how this evidence supports your argument. Each body paragraph needs:

- a strong **topic sentence** (usually the first sentence) that states the main point being made in the paragraph
- **evidence** from the text, including some brief quotations
- **analysis** of the textual evidence, with **explanation** of its significance and how it supports your argument
- **links back to the topic** in one or more statements, usually towards the end of the paragraph.

Connect the body paragraphs so that your discussion flows smoothly. Use some linking words and phrases such as 'similarly' and 'on the other hand', though don't start every paragraph like this. Another strategy is to use a significant word from the last sentence of one paragraph in the first sentence of the next.

Use key terms from the topic – or synonyms for them – throughout, so the relevance of your discussion to the topic is always clear.

The conclusion ties everything together and finishes the essay. It includes strong statements that emphasise your central argument and provide a clear response to the topic.

Avoid simply restating the points made earlier in the essay – this will end on a very flat note and imply that you have run out of ideas and vocabulary. The conclusion should be a logical extension of what you have written, not just a repetition or summary of it. Writing an effective conclusion can be a challenge. Try using these tips:

- Start by linking back to the final sentence of the second-last paragraph, rather than leaping to your main contention straight away – this helps your writing to flow.
- Use synonyms and expressions with equivalent meanings to vary your vocabulary. This allows you to reinforce your line of argument without being repetitive.
- When planning your essay, think of one or two broad statements or observations about the text's wider meaning. These should be related to the topic and your overall argument. Keep them for the conclusion, since they will give you something 'new' to say but still follow logically from your discussion. The introduction will be focused on the topic, but the conclusion can present a wider view of the text.

Essay topics

1 'Love looks not with the eyes, but with the mind …' (1.1.234)
Does the play confirm Helena's view, or challenge it?

2 *A Midsummer Night's Dream* affirms the importance of dreams and fantasy.
To what extent do you agree?

3 Although the female characters in *A Midsummer Night's Dream* try to assert themselves, it is the male characters who are in control.
Discuss.

4 *A Midsummer Night's Dream* suggests that humans are essentially inconstant.
Discuss.

5 To what extent does the play succeed in harmonising reason and love?
Discuss.

6 It is fitting that Puck concludes the play.
Do you agree?

7 'As she is mine, I may dispose of her …' (1.1.42)
Although Theseus supports Egeus' point of view, the play as a whole does not.
Discuss.

8 *A Midsummer Night's Dream* is an entertaining comedy with a significant darker side.
Discuss.

9 How does the Mechanicals' performance of 'Pyramus and Thisbe' add to the exploration of ideas in *A Midsummer Night's Dream*?

10 *A Midsummer Night's Dream* suggests that individuals don't have complete control over their lives.
Discuss.

11 What role does transformation play in *A Midsummer Night's Dream*?

Vocabulary for writing on the play

Comedy: a dramatic genre in which the main characters face conflicts and challenges, but all ends happily. Shakespearean comedies typically end with one or more weddings and a sense of renewal.

Iambic pentameter: a rhythmic pattern in poetry in which a ten-syllable line has alternating weak and strong beats. It is the main rhythmic pattern in Shakespearean drama when the characters speak in verse. An example is Hippolyta's first line (the bold syllables are accented or stressed):

> Four **days** will **quick**ly **steep** them**selves** in **night** …

Pastoral: a literary genre that depicts rural life, especially with shepherds; often presents an idealised view.

Prose: the use of language without regular rhythm or rhyme. The Mechanicals talk to one another in prose, setting them apart from the members of Theseus' court who speak in verse.

Rhyme: matching sounds at the ends of lines. Shakespeare often ends scenes with rhyming couplets. For example, these lines by Helena conclude the opening scene:

> But herein mean I to enrich my pain,
> To have his sight thither, and back again. (1.1.250–1)

Trochaic tetrameter: a rhythmic pattern in which an eight-syllable line has alternating strong and weak beats. In *A Midsummer Night's Dream* it often has the last syllable missing, as in these lines by Titania:

> **Hand** in **hand** with **fair**y **grace**
> **Will** we **sing** and **bless** this **place**. (5.1.377–8)

Oberon and Puck also use this metre when chanting spells, and Puck uses it in his epilogue:

> **If** we **shad**ows **have** of**fen**ded … (5.1.401)

Analysis of a sample topic

What role does transformation play in *A Midsummer Night's Dream*?

A topic like this invites a broad response, as it asks you to consider one of the key themes in the play. This gives you freedom to select the areas you focus on and the conclusions you draw.

Pay close attention to key words. Here, the obvious theme word is 'transformation', so you are invited to explore the various transformations in the play, including character transitions, events that mark significant developments, and even imagery relating to change.

You should also pay attention to the phrase 'what role', and ensure that you examine *how* these transformations connect to other themes, illustrate characters and relationships, create a mood and develop the narrative.

Possible contentions could include the following.

- 'By foregrounding moments of change and transition in *A Midsummer Night's Dream*, Shakespeare illustrates how impermanent and subjective human experience can be.'
- 'The play's exploration of transformation provides a structure for the characters' journeys.'
- 'In *A Midsummer Night's Dream*, transformation is shown to be central to life.'

The following sample analysis uses the third contention above.

Sample introduction

> Transformation is omnipresent in the play, and is shown to have both negative and positive consequences. It is also shown to be unavoidable, across both human and fairy realms. Whether it takes the form of growth or of transitions between different states of being, change is represented as a fundamental element of all journeys. The transformations in *A Midsummer Night's Dream* contribute to narrative conflicts and tensions and also facilitate the ultimate resolutions and happy endings.

Body paragraph outline

Paragraph 1: define transformation; explain how it is present on every level of the play.

- Aspects evident in the play include transitions from one state to another, disguises, altered feelings, shifts in location/context and rearranged love-pairings.
- The 'love-in-idleness' flower (2.1.168) is an agent of transformation and underlies main events / changing relationships.
- The play moves between the court and the wood, showing two worlds.
- The play-within-a-play shows people disguising/altering identity (linked with Bottom's unintended 'disguise' as an ass).
- The fairy characters (especially Puck and Oberon) have power to change humans' realities.
- Puck's speeches 'sometime lurk I' (from 2.1.47) and 'sometime a horse I'll be' (from 3.1.90) illustrate transformation (for him specifically, but also reminding us that all life is in flux).

Paragraph 2: transformation can be threatening/distressing/dangerous.

- When Bottom reappears after Puck places the ass head on him, the others are frightened because he is 'changed' (3.1.96) and 'translated' (3.1.98).
- The Mechanicals reassure the audience that their transitions into character roles are not real or permanent.
- Titania and Oberon's quarrel (and resulting change in relationship) unsettles the balance of the natural world, as outlined in Titania's Act 2 monologue cataloguing the 'progeny of evils' (2.1.115).

Paragraph 3: transformation can be desirable and beneficial.

- Helena wants to become an imitation of Hermia so Demetrius might love her; she wishes: 'My ear should catch your voice, my eye your eye, / My tongue should catch your tongue's sweet melody' (1.1.188–9).

- Hippolyta is impatient for the moon to change; she declares, 'I am aweary of this moon. Would he would change!' (5.1.238) in relation to Starveling's performance, which also hints at her desire to transition into the next phase of life.
- Oberon uses the love juice to restore Titania's affection and to resolve their quarrel (though note that while this is beneficial for him it could be viewed as unfair to her).
- Context can change experience. For Helena, Demetrius has power to make things better in her world: 'It is not night when I do see your face' (2.1.221). Hermia also notes that perception is altered by context: 'Dark night, that from the eye his function takes, / The ear more quick of apprehension makes' (3.2.177–8).
- Love can be transformative: 'Things base and vile, holding no quantity, / Love can transpose to form and dignity' (Helena, 1.1.232–3).

Sample conclusion

> Just as a writer creates something from nothing – 'the poet's pen / ... gives to airy nothing / A local habitation and a name' (5.1.15–17) – so change can create opportunities or pose obstacles, shape destinies or ensure happily-ever-afters. *A Midsummer Night's Dream* shows that no aspect of life is untouched by transformation. Love affairs wax and wane, theatrical performances and magical juices allow for temporary transitions, and circumstances alter perception. Through it all, change remains the only constant.

SAMPLE ANSWER

How does Shakespeare use pairs and opposites to explore ideas in *A Midsummer Night's Dream*?

Shakespeare's *A Midsummer Night's Dream* is built on binaries and parallels, at all levels – from plot to character to language choices. Pairs and opposites are used to illustrate both differences and similarities, by linking contrasting or similar characters and ideas. The various forms of pairing and opposition facilitate explorations of themes, including those of conflict and harmony (themselves a binary pair). By constructing a world in which we often see two characters or ideas in antipathy, Shakespeare illustrates how such discord can be resolved, and ultimately the play shows that through pairing (particularly in love), harmony and balance may be restored.

In the play, binaries are created between characters, between settings and between concepts. For example, there are several pairs of lovers: Theseus/Hippolyta; Oberon/Titania; the various couplings among Lysander, Demetrius, Hermia and Helena; Pyramus/Thisbe. These pairs illustrate a view of humanity in which partnership is an essential aspect of life, with Puck's prediction that 'Jack shall have Jill … and all shall be well' suggesting the importance of romantic couplings. These relationships develop within a distinct pair of settings – the court (a place of order, convention and reason) and the wood (a place of magic, unpredictability and dreams) – with this contrast revealing two equally necessary sides of life. Coupled characters also include those not in love, such as childhood friends Helena and Hermia; the trickster partnership of Oberon and Puck; and the parallel characters Demetrius and Lysander competing for the same woman's affections.

The paired concepts associated with these relationships and settings include love and hate; reality and illusion; and human and non-human (including the fairy world and Bottom's time as an ass). Another key binary underlying the central plot of the young lovers is that of male and female. In this play Shakespeare suggests that constancy in love is a gendered issue: both Lysander and Demetrius shift their affections, while Hermia and Helena never do. Other paired concepts in the play include age and youth (Theseus and Hippolyta compared with the younger lovers); being awake and 'dreaming' (including the fairy-altered states and Hermia's actual nightmare); and even shortness and tallness – Hermia accuses Helena of having 'made compare / Between our statures', and several of the insults they exchange are based on their differing heights.

At the language level, imagery often emphasises a pairing or opposition explored more literally in the play, such as Helena's 'Your vows to her and me, put in two scales, / Will even weigh', which points to the idea of balance and possibly even justice. Other imagery creates links and contrasts through juxtaposition, such as when Theseus, introducing the Interlude, marvels at the paradox of 'hot ice and wondrous strange snow' and ponders how to find 'the concord of this discord'. These phrases bring opposites together and point to differences being reconciled, thus foreshadowing the eventual happy ending.

At times Shakespeare relies on parallels to show how conflict or opposition can exist between two individuals or two concepts. Most obviously this is illustrated in Demetrius and Lysander's competition for the same woman (first Hermia, and then, in the wood, Helena). The two men are matched in rivalry to the point of wanting (albeit manipulated by Puck) to fight. The young women, too, have a bitter skirmish, despite their deep childhood friendship: 'As if our hands, our sides, voices, and minds / Had been incorporate … / Like to a double cherry'. When love is at stake (and Puck has caused chaos), their childhood closeness is diametrically opposed to the hostility of their argument, in which Hermia even threatens to scratch Helena's eyes. The conflict between Oberon and Titania – a powerfully symbolic couple as the king and queen of fairyland – disturbs the natural world (their 'brawls' cause wild weather). Even the history between Hippolyta and Theseus is marred by conflict, with Shakespeare acknowledging the mythological battle between their peoples in Theseus' 'I wooed thee with my sword'.

However, these instances of competition or conflict are all shown to be transient and to lead ultimately to harmony, marked by the romantic pairings of all the couples. The harmony between 'the pairs of faithful lovers' at the conclusion of the play is one of the strongest ways in which Shakespeare uses coupling and duality to show the importance of balance in the world. All the main characters are happily paired or reunited by the final scene, with each pair to become 'two bosoms interchainèd with an oath'. This neat resolution, in contrast to the mistakes and chaos that have played out, is fitting for the play's comic genre. As Puck says in his closing speech, any conflict (indeed the play itself) has been 'but a dream' and now 'all is mended'. The fairy world is reconciled; hate has been replaced by love; and any disconnection between reality and fantasy has been removed.

After the couples wake from their night's enchantments, Hermia thinks 'everything seems double', which ostensibly refers to the haze of dreamlike memory of what they have experienced. However, we can also read this as a reminder of how pairs and opposites inform so much of *A Midsummer Night's Dream*, illuminating difference and similarity, conflict and resolution. The 'double' vision Hermia experiences refers not just to the intangible magic that has affected them all, but also to the essential dualities of ideas in the world.

REFERENCES & READING

Text

Shakespeare, W 2014, *A Midsummer Night's Dream*, ed. L Buckle, Cambridge School Shakespeare series, Cambridge University Press, Cambridge.

References and further reading

Barber, CL 1959, *Shakespeare's Festive Comedy*, Princeton University Press, Princeton.

Brugger, W 2006, 'Bottom gets a life: Michael Hoffman's contribution to the Shakespeare film canon', *Journal of the Wooden O*, vol. 6, pp.1–15, available at https://omeka.li.suu.edu/ojs/index.php/woodeno/article/view/122/102

Dutton, R (ed.) 1996, *A Midsummer Night's Dream*, New Casebooks, Bloomsbury Publishing, New York.

Hatfull, R 2019, '"Keeping the dream alive": Nicholas Hytner's *A Midsummer Night's Dream*', *Critical Insights*, pp.208–24, available at https://warwick.ac.uk/fac/arts/scapvc/theatre/staff/ronanhatfull/pages_from_a_midsummer_nights_dream_c.pdf

Kott, J 1964, *Shakespeare, Our Contemporary*, trans. B Taborski, WW Norton & Company, New York.

Mandel, J 1973, 'Dream and imagination in Shakespeare', *Shakespeare Quarterly*, vol. 24, no. 1, pp.61–8.

Miller, RF 1975, '*A Midsummer Night's Dream*: the fairies, bottom, and the mystery of things', *Shakespeare Quarterly*, vol. 26, no. 3, pp.254–68.

Nashe, T 1594, *The Terrors of the Night; Or, A Discourse of Apparitions*, www.oxford-shakespeare.com/Nashe/Terrors_Night.pdf

Schalkwyk, D 1986, 'The role of imagination in *A Midsummer Night's Dream*', *Theoria: A Journal of Social and Political Theory*, no. 66, pp.51–65.

Scot, R 1886, *The Discoverie of Witchcraft*, first published 1584, available at https://archive.org/details/discoverieofwitc00scot/mode/2up

Walters, L 2016, 'Monstrous births and imaginations: authorship and folklore in Shakespeare's *A Midsummer Night's Dream*', *Renaissance and Reformation*, vol. 39, no. 1, Winter, pp.115–46.

Online film resources

The following productions at the Shakespeare's Globe theatre can be viewed on the Globe Player at https://player.shakespearesglobe.com:

- 2013 directed by Dominic Dromgoole
- 2016 directed by Emma Rice (Bollywood inspired)
- 2021 directed by Sean Holmes

The 1968 film directed by Peter Hall is also available on YouTube at https://www.youtube.com/watch?v=F9Ry0lUghcw

The 1999 film directed by Michael Hoffman is available through streaming services.